To Ge[...]

On the [...] of your

christening,

Sunday 24th October 2010.

Lots of love.

Grandpa and Nana.

ꞋIllustrated꞉
ꞋBook of
Nature

First published in 2009 by Usborne Publishing Ltd.,
Usborne House, 83-85 Saffron Hill, London, EC1N 8RT, England
www.usborne.com

Printed in Dubai

Illustrated Book of Nature

Phillip Clarke, Laura Howell and Sarah Khan

Designed by Joanne Kirkby, Michael Hill,
Kate Rimmer, Laura Hammonds,
Marc Maynard and Nayera Everall

Digital manipulation by Keith Furnival

Consultants: Katherine Kear, Derek Niemann, Derek Patch,
Dr Margaret Rostron, Jenny Steel and Dr Roger Trend

Edited by Kirsteen Rogers

Usborne Quicklinks

The Usborne Quicklinks Website is packed with thousands of links to all the best websites on the internet. The websites include information, video clips, sounds, games and animations that support and enhance the information in Usborne internet-linked books.

To visit the recommended websites for the Illustrated Book of Nature, go to the Usborne Quicklinks Website at **www.usborne-quicklinks.com** and enter the keywords: **illustrated nature**

Pictures to download

You can download many of the pictures in this book from the Usborne Quicklinks Website. These pictures are for personal use only and must not be used for commercial purposes.

Internet safety

When using the internet please follow the internet safety guidelines displayed on the Usborne Quicklinks Website. The websites recommended in Usborne Quicklinks are regularly reviewed. However, the content of a website may change at any time and Usborne Publishing is not responsible for the content of websites other than its own. We recommend that children are supervised while on the internet.

Contents

Trees

Flowers

Seashore

Garden wildlife

Watching wildlife

In the countryside, at the beach, or even in a park or garden – you will find animals, plants and trees in all kinds of places if you stay on the lookout.

Being prepared

For a nature-spotting trip away from home, it's best to wear layers of light, waterproof clothing that covers your arms and legs. Never go out on your own, and make sure you tell someone where you're going to be.

Staying quiet and hidden will help you spot shyer animals, such as these deer.

A low profile

Animals can be nervous, so might be startled by bright colours and loud noises. If you want to get a close look at animals, try wearing dull colours, and staying in sheltered spots. Some places have purpose-built hides and viewing points from where you might see the local wildlife.

You might find a hide from which you can watch water birds, such as herons.

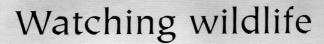

Taking pictures

Making a photo album is a fun way to keep a record of the wildlife you've seen. Here are some tips on how to take a good nature picture:

If you use a ring binder, you can keep adding to the album.

The photographer used his camera's zoom function to get this close-up picture.

• Keep the sun behind you and make sure your shadow doesn't fall across your subject.

• Try using your camera's zoom function to get a close-up picture.

• If there isn't much light, you can use the camera's flash, but avoid it if you're photographing animals.

• If a flower is difficult to see amongst leaves or grass, place a piece of card behind it to make a plain background.

Respecting nature

When out and about in the countryside, always remember to follow this code:

• Never light fires

• Keep to paths, and close gates behind you

• Keep dogs under control

• Don't damage hedges, fences, walls or signs

• Look, don't touch: leave plants, animals and nests alone

• Take your litter home with you

Birds

About birds

You can find birds soaring through the air, singing in treetops or even gliding through water. There are 10,000 kinds of bird and probably more yet to be discovered.

What makes a bird a bird?

Even the tiniest hummingbird and the tallest ostrich have features in common. Like all birds, they have one beak, two legs and wings, and hundreds of feathers. They also hatch from eggs and can keep their bodies at a constant temperature.

Colourful Eurasian nuthatches are stout birds with thick legs and feet.

Europe's smallest bird, goldcrests are quiet and unassuming, with thin legs and dull feathers, apart from a yellow head stripe.

American northern cardinals are loud and flashy, with a distinctive crest of feathers on the top of their heads.

Early birds

Scientists think that the first birds appeared 145 million years ago, at the time of the dinosaurs. As well as having feathers and wings like modern birds, these prehistoric creatures also possessed sharp teeth and long, bony tails.

Today's birds are descended from feathered prehistoric creatures, such as this Archaeopteryx.

Where birds live

Birds are skilled survivors that have adapted to live in all types of environments – from lush tropical rainforests to freezing polar ice caps. The varied landscapes of Europe are home to over 500 species of bird.

Magpies fly from tree to tree in parks and gardens.

Puffins nest on towering cliffs.

Blackbirds sing from branches on farmland and in woods.

Mallards splash about in ponds and lakes.

Changing places

The particular surroundings a bird lives in, such as farmland or marshes, are called its habitat. As the seasons change, some birds change habitats. Others always choose the same kind of habitat, even if they spend different seasons in different countries.

This exotic-looking grassland bird is a hoopoe. Like many hoopoes, it divides its time between the open, grassy plains of Africa and the green fields of Europe.

Top to toe

Although birds all have the same basic shape and body parts, the closer you look, the more fascinating variations you'll soon spot.

Winging it

Whether a bird mainly flits, swoops or soars depends on its wing design. Even the movement of some flightless birds, such as penguins, can be affected by the shape and size of their wings.

Curved, pointed wings help swallows speed like arrows through the air.

Eagles keep their broad wings stretched out to glide on the breeze.

Legs and feet

When on land and in the water, birds rely on their legs and feet, not only to keep them moving, but often also to keep them safe and fed. The length and form of their limbs are suited to the jobs they need to do.

Strong, muscly feet help ptarmigans scratch in the ice and snow to uncover seeds and insects.

Sedge warblers have flexible toes, with one pointing backwards, which is ideal for grasping perches.

Long legs help wading birds, like this stilt, to keep their feathers dry while searching for food in deep water.

Balancing acts

A bird's tail helps it to stay balanced when on its feet, and whilst in the air, too. In flight, a bird also "steers" with its tail, adjusting the angle of it to change direction.

Long-tailed tits tilt their tails as they flit from tree to tree.

As they climb, woodpeckers hold their strong, stiff tails against a tree trunk for stability.

A wagtail's long tail helps it make sharp turns as it chases agile insects across the sky.

Beaks and bills

Birds' beaks take the place of a whole drawerful of kitchen utensils, handling food in various ways. Depending on their shape, beaks can be used for picking food up, cracking it open, sieving it from the water or ripping it apart.

A finch's cone-shaped beak is ideal for cracking open seeds.

Hooked beaks help kestrels to kill and tear up their prey.

Equipped with its long, jabbing beak, this black-tailed godwit can probe the muddy shore for insects and snails.

Dabbling ducks use their flat beaks to filter food from the water.

Fluff and feathers

Birds are the only animals with feathers. It's vital for a bird to take good care of them, as its feathery coat not only helps it to fly, but also protects it from the cold and rain.

Looking at feathers

Feathers are made of keratin, the same tough substance that makes up people's hair and nails. Every feather has a central tube-like shaft, with a flexible, soft part on either side, called a vane.

Goldfinch feather

Vane

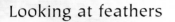

Shaft

Close-up

Shaft

Types of feathers

A bird has three types of feathers. A layer of fluffy down feathers next to its skin helps keep it warm. These are covered by sleek body feathers, which protect it from rain and wind. Stiff flight feathers on its wings and tail push down on the air to help it fly.

Down feather

Body feather

Flight feather

Adult goose

Body feathers

Flight feathers

As with all chicks, this baby goose's downy coat will be replaced with body feathers as it grows. It will still have a downy undercoat as an adult.

Taking a bath

Like people, birds bathe in water to keep clean; unlike people, many also take dust baths. They roll around on dry ground to remove lice and excess oil from their feathers. Some birds even rub ants onto their feathers, covering themselves in a lice-killing acid that the ants release from their bodies.

You might spot a bathing bird tumbling about on the dry earth...

...or making a splash in a puddle or stream.

Feather care

Birds comb their feathers with their beaks or feet. Most cover them with an oil squeezed from above their tails. This slippery goo makes their feathers waterproof and flexible, and also kills harmful germs.

Herons have a jagged edge on one of their claws, which they use like a comb to groom their feathers.

Dropping off

Birds moult regularly, shedding and replacing their damaged or worn feathers. The feathers don't drop off all at once, but over a few weeks or months. Different birds moult at different times of the year.

In summer, dunlins' feathers are brown and black.

In winter, the summer plumage is replaced by white and grey feathers.

Flying machines

When a bird flies, different parts of its body work together to keep it in the air. On the outside, its wings flap up and down, twisting to and fro, but there's lots going on inside, too.

Bones and muscles

To lift off the ground, birds must be strong, but light, too. Powerful chest muscles help them to beat their wings quickly, and hollow bones keep their bodies light. The bones are strengthened by a honeycomb-like mesh of thinner bone that supports them from the inside.

Hollow

Criss-cross lattice of inner bone

This diagram shows the large chest muscles that power an owl's wings.

Wing bones

Beneath the feathers and skin, a bird's wing has an elbow, wrist and fingers, similar to a person's arm and hand. These bones help birds to use their wings in different ways.

A peregrine falcon glides with its wings stretched out.

A swallow folds its wings back to swoop through the air.

As it hovers in search of prey, a kestrel holds its wings up.

Eye protection

As the air whistles past a flying bird, its eyes come under attack from dust, grit and drying winds. To protect them, birds have an extra, see-through eyelid, which they keep shut in flight.

How wings work

In flight, streams of air flow above and below a bird's wings. The front edge of each wing is curved on top, so the air above has to flow over this curve. For the two streams to meet at the back of the wing at the same time, the stream above has to flow faster than the one below. The faster moving stream presses down less than the lower one, which helps lift the bird up.

The difference in air pressure above and below this Arctic tern's wings helps it rise into the air.

Curved path of an air stream over a gull's wing

Power generators

Birds need a lot of energy to fly. Their hearts beat dozens of times quicker than people's hearts, to pump plenty of energy-releasing oxygen around their bodies. Smaller birds are often more active than larger ones, so their hearts beat faster still.

A chaffinch's heart can beat 1,000 times a minute.

Ravens' hearts beat more slowly, up to 600 times a minute.

Birds in flight

For birds, flying is a matter of co-ordination. Whether
they're taking off, landing or simply fluttering about, birds
need strength, precision and perfect timing.

Getting off the ground

To many birds, taking flight
means leaping up and flapping
their wings as fast as they can.
But some birds are too heavy
for these acrobatic starts. They
have to run along, flapping all
the while, until they're able
to rise into the air.

This big whooper
swan needs a long,
flappy run across the
water before take-off.

Figure of eight

Up and down wingbeats lift a bird up.
Once it's airborne, though, moving
forwards means changing the shape of
its wingbeats to a figure of eight pattern.

House sparrows flap
their wings more than
12 times a second in
fast flight.

The bird pushes
its wings down
and forwards.

As it sweeps its wings
up, it opens its feathers
to let air through.

When its wings are
fully raised, the bird
closes its feathers.

It then beats down
with its wings
once again.

Flight patterns

Birds don't always take the straightest path through the air. Next time you watch a bird in flight, try to imagine what pattern its path would make across the skies.

A buzzard holds out its wings to soar in a spiral on rising currents of warm air.

By flapping, then gliding on the air currents, a finch gently bounces along.

Skydivers

Some birds that hunt animals dive down from the sky to take their prey by surprise. They fold their wings back to dive, shaping their bodies like a streamlined arrow.

A goose flies fast and straight across the sky.

You might spot a streak of blue as a kingfisher dives into a river...

...or see a gannet plummeting unstoppably into the sea.

Coming in to land

Landing is a tricky manoeuvre. To land neatly where it wants to, a bird slows its wing beats and brings its feet forwards. Then, it lifts its wings and fans out its tail to catch the air, which slows it down enough to land safely.

Wings lifted

Tail spread out

Feet brought forwards

This starling is in position for an accurate landing.

On land and water

Few birds spend all their time in the air, so they have to be able to move around on land and, in some cases, through water too.

Looking at legs

At first glance, it looks as though birds' knees bend the opposite way to people's. In fact, the bends you can see are ankles. Their knees are higher up, usually hidden by feathers. Beneath the ankles are the feet, then the part that birds walk on – their toes.

To perch, this willow warbler bends its ankles, and its toes automatically curl around and lock to grip the twig.

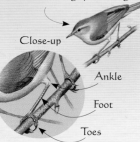

Close-up

Ankle

Foot

Toes

Step by step

On the ground, birds move mainly by hopping with both feet together or by walking, putting one foot out at a time. There's no hard and fast rule about which birds move in which way.

As you can see here, a pheasant struts, placing one foot directly in front of the other.

Although it can break out into a run, a blackbird usually hops with both feet together.

A pigeon strides along, moving its feet forwards alternately, like a person walking.

Creepers and climbers

Climbing birds, such as woodpeckers, hop or creep up tree trunks, gobbling up insects. Most birds have one toe pointing back and three pointing forward on each foot, but woodpeckers have two toes pointing in each direction. This helps them cling steadily onto the trunks.

A green woodpecker's toes can grip even the smoothest of trunks.

Walkers and waders

Birds that spend a lot of time on the ground tend to have long, splayed-out toes to help them balance. This also spreads their weight over the surface, so that they don't sink into soft ground.

A meadow pipit's long toes let it walk around on mushy ground without sinking.

Swimmers

Most water birds have flaps of skin, called webs, between their toes. As a bird swims, it kicks its feet and stretches out its toes, using the webs as paddles to propel itself forwards. When it brings its feet back, it closes its toes, so the webs don't drag through the water.

A shoveler's footprint shows full webbing.

The webs on a shoveler's feet completely fuse its toes together, giving it maximum paddling power.

A coot's footprint shows partial webbing.

A coot's webs don't join its toes fully, so it can move just as easily on land as it can through water.

Finding food

Birds are very active and require plenty of energy.
Needing food to fuel their busy lifestyles, they spend
much of their time looking for their next meal.

What's for dinner?

Birds eat an amazing variety of foods. Some
feed on pollen, nuts and seeds, while others
prefer insects, fish or small mammals. A
few even eat other birds. To drink, birds
sip water, or nectar from flowers.

Swifts hunt down
insects as they fly
through the air.

Fieldfares eat berries,
especially in the
winter months.

You might spot birds like this
mallard taking a mouthful of
water from a pond.

A fat worm makes a
delicious meal for
a hungry robin.

Avoiding competition

The shape of a bird's beak helps it
get to the type of food it needs. All
three seed-eaters shown on the right
have strong beaks to crack open
the shells of seeds and nuts. But
variations in their beak design
help them reach different
kinds of seeds, so they don't
compete for one food source.

Big, sturdy beaks help
hawfinches crack olive
and cherry stones.

Goldfinches find seeds by
poking their fine, pointed
beaks into thistles and teasels.

The overlapping tips of a crossbill's
beak help it split a fir cone's scales
and collect the seeds inside.

Smashing shells

Some birds feast on small shelled animals, such as snails and seaside creatures. To break open their body armour, gulls and song thrushes dash the creatures against hard rocks, over and over until their shells crack.

On rocky beaches, you might see gulls bashing shells against the stones.

Now this song thrush has found a good spot for shell smashing, it will return to the same place time and again.

Food crushers

Birds don't have teeth, so they can't chew their food, and instead, swallow it in chunks. These pass into a muscly pouch near the stomach, which squeezes and squashes them to a digestible mush. Some birds gobble up small stones which stay in the pouch and help grind up really tough pieces of food.

As turnstones look for food under rocks, they swallow a few pebbles to help their digestion.

Birds of prey

Birds of prey are meat-eaters that hunt live prey or scavenge from dead animals. Of all the birds, they're among the fastest fliers, with the sharpest senses and the sharpest claws.

Air attack

To catch their prey, some hunting birds dive down from the sky, spearing their victims with their deadly talons. They then use their strong, curved beaks to pick the flesh off their lifeless victim.

A diving peregrine falcon can reach speeds of up to 180kph (112mph) – that's almost as fast as a racing car.

This kestrel is flying across the sky but, when looking for prey, it stays still, hovering in the air.

From a distance

Flying high up in the air, most birds would have trouble spotting small animals scuttling about on the ground. But birds of prey have excellent vision – around eight times sharper than a person's – so can spot their prey from far away.

A buzzard can spot a rabbit on the ground from ½km (¼mile) away.

Going fishing

Ospreys hunt fish. When they spot one, they swoop down through the air, plunge their feet into the water and seize their prey. Fish are slippery, especially when they're struggling, but an osprey has stiff spines on its feet that it can dig in to make escape impossible.

An osprey hovers above the water, waiting to see a fish near the surface.

It grabs a fish, locking its feet around its wriggling body.

Silent killers

Many owls sweep down on their unsuspecting victims in silence. Their flight feathers have fluffy, fringed edges, which muffle their wingbeats.

The soft fringes of this tawny owl's feathers reduce noise as it flies.

Night hunters

Birds that hunt at night have sharp hearing and eyesight to help them detect their prey in the gloom. Owls have big ears that hear the slightest movements, and large eyes that let in as much light as possible.

Feathers form a disc on the front of the face to funnel sounds into the ears.

Eyes at the front of the head, to help in judging distances

Ear hidden under feathers

Hide and seek

Birds come in all colours and patterns. Whether they are bright or plain often depends on whether they need to blend in with the background or stand out from the crowd.

Blending in

In the nesting season, most females stay in one spot, sitting on their eggs to keep them warm. This makes them vulnerable to attack by predators such as foxes, cats, people, and even other birds. Many mother birds are coloured in a way that matches their surroundings.

The patchy markings on a ringed plover help to camouflage it against the pebbly beaches where it nests.

When a snipe senses a predator nearby...

...it puts its head down and tail up so its stripes blend in with the grass.

It's difficult for an enemy to spot this eagle owl against the leafy ground on which it's resting.

To avoid detection, ptarmigans alter their colour with the changing seasons.

Winter plumage

Summer feathers

Hidden in the sky

Have you ever noticed how many seabirds have white bellies? As they fly above the waves looking for food, the fish can't see them against the bright sky, so the birds can swoop down and take them by surprise.

Camouflaged against the sky, these herring gulls soar above the seas and oceans, on the look-out for fish.

Identifying marks

Markings and colour can help a group of birds to stay together. Some geese, for example, use their distinctive markings to stay in sight of each other when they're flying in flocks over long distances.

Guided by the black and white rump of the bird in front, greylag geese follow the leader across the sky.

Look at me

To help them attract a mate, a male's feathers are often brighter than a female's. Some have eye-catching colours all year round, and others only develop fancy plumage when it's time to breed.

A female common pheasant's feathers are dull.

Male common pheasants have red patches around their eyes all year round.

In the breeding season, a male ruff grows feathery tufts around its head and neck. Later, the tufts fall out, and plain feathers grow back.

Male ruff in breeding season

Male after breeding season

You can tell whether a bullfinch is male or female by looking at the colour of its body.

Male

Female

Song and dance

Like people, birds have their own languages to communicate with each other. They use unique combinations of sounds and body language to get their message across.

Love songs

Birds sing most often when they're trying to find a mate. It's usually the males that perform, wooing females with ballads that can carry over long distances.

Cuckoos are named after their falling two-note song.

Nightingale songs are a melodious mix of trills, whistles and gurgles.

Male pigeons bow and coo loudly to court females.

Keep out

Love songs not only attract females, but also warn other males to stay away. If this doesn't work, and the rivals come face to face, a bird might perform a threatening display in an attempt to scare its enemy away.

Male European robins puff out their red breasts to threaten their rivals.

Copy-cat calls

Birds call out to give warnings, or to find each other. As chicks, some learn how to call by copying the sounds their parents make. Some birds can even mimic other animals, and machines.

Starlings can imitate anything from bleating sheep to ringing telephones.

Showing off

Many male birds show off to females by fluffing up their feathers, fanning out their tails, or stamping their feet in elaborate dances. In some species, the female joins in the dance, too.

Male and female grebes dance together by waggling their heads at each other...

...pulling up weeds...

...then, offering them to each other as tokens of commitment.

Putting on an act

As well as singing and dancing, some birds can act, too. Pretending to be injured, they limp along to lead predators away from their nests. Once at a safe distance, the "invalid" miraculously recovers and flies away.

A little ringed plover holds out its "broken" wing to attract a predator's attention.

Nest-builders

Once they've found a mate, most birds start making nests for the female to lay eggs inside. Many build from scratch, using materials they find lying around.

Building supplies

In spring, you'll often see busy birds flying to and fro collecting bits of twig or grass. You can help them by hanging up scraps of wool, dog hair or straw from a tree for them to use.

A few beakfuls of fluffy animal hair will help this blue tit to line its nest.

Rooks break off large twigs to make their nests.

A safe haven

Birds build nests anywhere that's safe from predators, often choosing places that are high above the ground or inside some kind of shelter. In winter, you can look in bare trees for nests that were used the previous summer.

Razorbills lay their eggs and raise their chicks on cliff ledges.

Sand martins dig out holes in sand banks to nest in.

Nest construction

Although birds' nests come in different shapes and sizes, most are circular. Birds weave the building materials together, constructing first the base, then the walls. As a finishing touch, they might line the nest with soft feathers or springy moss.

Long-tailed tits' nests are hollow balls made from lichens, moss, spiders' webs and feathers.

The feathers in this swallow's nest are keeping its eggs warm.

Using the grasses that grow by the water, coots weave their bowl-shaped nests on the edges of riverbanks.

Space invaders

Cuckoos don't bother to build nests of their own, but lay their eggs in other birds' nests. When the baby cuckoo hatches, it shoves the other eggs and young out of the nest, so its foster parents can fully devote themselves to raising the intruder.

A female cuckoo removes an egg from a reed warbler's nest and lays its own egg in its place.

The newly hatched cuckoo heaves out the other eggs.

The unsuspecting reed warbler parent works hard to feed the enormous cuckoo chick.

Eggs

An egg provides food and security for the baby bird forming inside it. Its structure, shape and even its colour are all designed to keep the developing chick safe.

Inside an egg

Within an egg's hard shell, floats the baby bird, cushioned by egg white and yolk. The white and yolk are food and water for the chick, and contain everything it needs to grow strong enough eventually to break out.

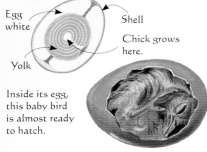

Egg white

Shell

Chick grows here.

Yolk

Inside its egg, this baby bird is almost ready to hatch.

Egg identification

The shell not only protects the growing chick but often makes it recognizable, too. The colours and markings on some eggshells help parent birds to identify their eggs.

Guillemots nest in large groups. They lay eggs in a vast array of shades and patterns, so parents can tell which are theirs.

Blending in

The colour of some birds' eggs helps them to blend into their surroundings, hiding them from predators. Some sea birds lay their eggs in dips on pebbly beaches. The eggs' stony hues and blotchy patterns make them difficult for enemies to spot.

The markings of this little tern's egg help to camouflage it on the shingly shore.

Egg-shaped

Most eggs are oval, and are narrower at one end than the other. If knocked, an oval egg spins in a tight circle instead of rolling away from its mother or out of the nest. Birds that lay directly onto cliff ledges tend to have longer and narrower eggs, so they don't roll down the perilous slopes.

Song thrush egg

Razorbills' eggs are laid on cliffsides, so are more pointed than the others shown here.

Spotted flycatcher eggs

Little owl egg

Sitting tight

Before their eggs are laid, some parent birds shed feathers from their bellies. After laying, they sit with the bare skin, called a brood patch, covering the eggs, to keep them warm.

This marsh tit keeps all its eggs cosy with one brood patch, but some birds have many patches – one for each egg.

This kittiwake is turning round to get comfortable in its nest, as it has to sit in the same spot for long periods of time until its chick hatches out.

Growing up

A chick emerges from its shell tired, hungry and often helpless. Over the next few weeks, it must gain the strength and skill it needs to face the world alone.

Breaking free

When it's time for a chick to hatch out, it begins chipping away at the inside of its shell using a tiny bump, called an egg tooth, on the tip of its beak. While the chick is busy tapping, it calls out to let its parents know that it's on its way.

The chick uses its egg tooth to poke a small hole in the shell.

Gradually, it chips all the way around the egg.

Finally, the chick forces the egg apart.

Busy parents

Baby birds have enormous appetites, so parents might spend several weeks travelling back and forth from their nests, bringing food for them. Some swallow the food they collect. When they return, they cough it up for the chicks to eat.

You might spot a bird flying back to its nest with an insect in its mouth.

The bright insides of these baby song thrushes' mouths show their parents where to drop the food.

First flights

At only a few weeks old, many chicks are strong enough to hop a little way from their nest. By copying their parents and following their own instincts, the chicks learn how to turn their clumsy hops into short flights, and then into longer voyages.

These fluffy robin chicks are strong enough to venture out of their nest, but not yet old enough to fly.

Before trying to take off, a young blue tit practises flapping whilst safely perched.

Taking to the water

Many water bird chicks can swim almost as soon as they hatch out. They usually stay close to an adult at first. If they become cold or tired, they might take a break and let their parent ferry them around on its back.

Mallard ducklings following their mother

Baby grebes hitching a ride from their father

Living together

Some birds keep themselves to themselves, only pairing up once a year to breed. But others eat, sleep and nest in huge groups, living together for long periods of time.

Pecking order

To stop squabbling within a flock, many large groups of birds rank their members according to how aggressive they are. The top birds are the most savage, and they get first choice of food and territory.

...and give loud calls to show how fierce they can be.

Gulls ferociously rip out pieces of grass from the ground...

Cliff colonies

For most of the year, many sea birds live out at sea, swooping over the oceans and bobbing about on the waves. In spring, they come to the shore to find a mate and raise their chicks. They settle on cliff ledges in huge groups called colonies.

There can be thousands of birds in a single cormorant colony.

Two-thirds of the world's gannets nest in groups on cliffs and rocky outcrops in the UK.

Safety in numbers

As winter approaches, the weather grows colder and food becomes scarce. Some birds that live alone during the rest of the year flock together in the winter months to keep warm, find food and watch out for predators.

Long-tailed tits gather in family groups of brothers, sisters, parents and grandparents.

On a snowy lawn in winter, a flock of feeding greenfinches is joined by a hungry sparrow.

Tree sparrow

Team work

Some shore birds hunt in gangs. On muddy beaches, you might see gaggles of geese searching for food or flocks of knots lined up in rows, moving forward together, poking the ground with their beaks as they go.

Brent geese flock together to feed in winter – some search for food, while others act as sentries, keeping a look-out for predators.

Long journeys

Every year, millions of birds migrate vast distances to search for food and places to breed. Some also make these long and dangerous journeys to escape harsh weather conditions.

Fuel for the journey

Some birds travel thousands of miles, making no or very few stops. So that they don't starve on the way, many eat as much as they can for a few weeks before they set out. Others eat on the wing or make frequent feeding stops on the way.

Crossing the globe on their long trips from the Arctic to the Antarctic and back again, Arctic terns only make short stops to eat.

Migrating swallows gobble up flying insects along the way.

Garden warblers can eat enough to double their body weight before they leave, to allow them to cross the Sahara desert non-stop.

During migration, large birds, such as white storks, take regular but short snack breaks – they have to watch their weight so they don't become too heavy to fly.

Night flights

Many migrating birds don't make much progress during daylight hours, using this time to rest and eat. They do most of their flying at night, as the air is cooler and the winds are less blustery after dark.

During the day, you might see a flock of migrating birds resting on overhead wires, waiting for nightfall.

Sticking together

Birds often migrate in groups rather than fly solo, as a bird's chances of surviving a predator's attack are greater if it's part of a flock. You might spot migrating birds flying in huge masses or in smaller formations.

When the leader of this flock of whooper swans gets tired, one of the others will take over the lead.

Following the signs

Scientists don't fully understand how birds can navigate over such massive distances, but they have come up with a few theories. Some species might use a combination of these methods.

Shelducks fly in a "V" shape, after a leader.

Ospreys and other birds that migrate during the day might follow landmarks, such as mountains and islands.

The position of the Moon and stars may help redwings and other night-fliers to find their way.

Research on pigeons suggests that they are guided by lines of magnetic forces from the centre of the Earth.

Fast asleep

Like all animals, birds get tired and fall asleep. They don't doze for long though, taking only short naps so they can avoid predators and keep from freezing in cold weather.

Huge groups of starlings roost in trees.

Half awake

Birds can literally sleep with one eye open, and with half of their brain awake, too. This lets them watch for predators whilst also getting some rest. While they sleep, birds don't go limp and floppy, like people do, but stay upright.

Hot spots

Many birds sleep huddled together in groups called roosts, warmed by each other's body heat. Birds that sleep alone look for cosy places to bed down, in tangled undergrowth, or crevices under roofs and in walls.

As a brambling sleeps, its legs stiffen and toes lock around its twiggy perch.

Fulmars fold their legs underneath them to rest on cliff ledges.

On cold nights, you might see wrens squeezing into bushes to roost.

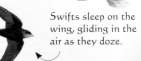

Swifts sleep on the wing, gliding in the air as they doze.

Tucking up

At night, the parts of a bird's body that aren't covered in feathers are particularly vulnerable to the cold. To keep them warm, birds can tuck their beaks into their shoulder feathers or hold one leg up against their bodies.

Waterbirds like these can sleep standing up, with one foot tucked up to their bellies.

Golden plover

Canada goose

This male tufted duck is keeping both its beak and foot warm as it sleeps.

Fluffing out

When it's very cold, you might spot a bird sleeping with its feathers all fluffed up. This traps tiny pockets of air next to its skin. The air is heated by the warmth of the bird's body and stops its body heat escaping.

These feathery mounds are sparrows, sleeping with their feathers raised and beaks tucked in.

Even when curled up into a fluffy ball to sleep, this blue tit can stay balanced on the thinnest of twigs.

Up at night

As night falls, most birds settle down to sleep but, for a few, dusk is the start of their day. These nocturnal birds spend the daytime dozing, but perk up when the Sun starts to set.

Sharp senses

Nocturnal birds have excellent vision and hearing, which help them to find food in the dark. Even on the gloomiest nights, some owls can see a mouse moving from 2m (6ft) away, and hear it rustling in the grass from an even greater distance.

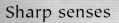

Of all the European owls, tawny owls can spot their prey in the dimmest light.

Swooping down on its prey, this barn owl is using its super senses to pinpoint the exact position of its target.

Barn owl   Short-eared owl

Owls can twist their heads around and even upside down.

Turning heads

Owls have big eyes to help their night sight. In fact, their eyeballs are so huge that they can hardly move them, so they turn their whole heads instead. An owl's neck is very flexible, allowing it to swivel its head in all directions.

Reflecting light

Even birds with smaller eyes can have keen night vision. Nightjars hunt for insects in the evenings, and have shiny layers at the back of their eyeballs to reflect light onto light-sensitive areas of their eyes. This helps them to see their tiny prey in the dim twilight.

Bristles around a nightjar's mouth help it to direct insects into its open beak.

Night calls

Nocturnal birds are often quite difficult to spot but, in the evenings, you can listen out for them calling to each other.

Little owls, like this one, make a mewing sound. Barn owls screech, and long- and short-eared owls hoot. A tawny owl calls out "te-wit", and another answers "te-woo".

Storm petrels purr and cluck around their coastal breeding grounds at night.

Water rails make pig-like squeals and grunts as they skulk about in clumps of reeds at twilight.

Day disguise

Roosting in broad daylight, nocturnal birds are vulnerable to attack from predators. Many have brown and grey feathers, to camouflage them against the trees or forest floors where they sleep.

It's hard to spot a woodcock resting among the dead leaves that carpet its woodland home.

Birdwatching

Birdwatching can be as easy as finding a quiet spot and seeing what birds are around. But a little planning and a few basic pieces of equipment can make it much more fun.

Where to watch

Some birds are most likely to be seen in particular habitats. For example, swans can be found on lakes and rivers, and grouse on moors and mountains. A few birds don't mind people near them, but most are shy, so it's best to watch them quietly, from a place where they can't see you.

You don't have to hide to watch robins, as they are bold near people...

...but less confident birds like these blackcaps may hide or fly off if they sense that a person is close by.

Female

Male

When to watch

Certain times are better than others for birdwatching. You're more likely to spot birds in the morning than in the evening, and in spring and autumn than in summer or winter. But, no matter what time of day or year it is, there's always something to see.

These birds visit Europe in spring.

Common tern

Chiffchaff

Sanderlings are winter visitors to Europe.

It's easier to sketch a bird if it's perched, or standing still on the ground.

Making notes

You could keep a record of the birds you've spotted by making sketches and jotting down when and where you saw them. If you don't recognize a bird, you could make notes about it, then look it up later in a field guide like the one shown at the bottom of this page.

These are the kinds of things that you could note down.

Black head

White collar

8th June
Near canal
Weather - sunny
2:30pm

Dark throat

Sparrow-like body

Perched on tree branch

Bouncing flight pattern

Sketching birds

1. Start with circles for the head and body.

2. Draw lines for the neck, beak, tail and legs.

3. Add details, such as markings or a crest on the head.

Using a field guide

Field guides are books packed with pictures and descriptions of birds, their habitats and behaviour. Some are bulky reference books; others are small enough to slip into a pocket or bag when you go out birdwatching.

With a field guide, you could work out that the bird at the top of this page is a male reed bunting.

SPARROWS, BUNTINGS

HOUSE SPARROW
Very familiar bird. Lives near houses and even in city centres, where it eats scraps. Often seen in flocks. 15cm.

Male and female House Sparrow

TREE SPARROW
Usually nests in holes in trees or cliffs. Much less common than house sparrow. 14cm.

YELLOWHAMMER
Found in open country, especially farmland. Feeds on ground. Forms flocks in winter, sings from the tops of bushes. 17cm.

Male and female Yellowhammer

REED BUNTING
Most common near water, but some nest in dry areas with long grass. May visit bird tables in winter. 15cm.

CORN BUNTING
Nests in cornfields. Sings from posts, bushes or overhead wires. 18cm.

Feeding birds

You can help birds to survive when their natural food is scarce by putting out food in a garden. Offering a range of foods will attract a variety of birds for you to spot.

Feed the birds

Birds need food in every season, but winter and spring are the most important times to help them. It takes all their strength to cope with the cold weather, then raise chicks.

The food you put out in spring gives birds energy to fly around finding small animals to feed to their young.

Giving food

There are lots of ways to leave food out for birds. The simplest is to scatter it on the ground, but this isn't ideal, as it might attract rats. If you have space you could buy a bird table, or a feeder or two from a garden centre or hardware store.

Robin

Greenfinch

Blackbirds often visit tables, and they also like to hunt for earthworms in flowerbeds.

A handful of seeds quickly attracts birds to the table.

Dunnocks eat seeds that they find on the ground.

Types of feeders

To attract the most birds, use several feeders with different foods in each one. Hang them high off the ground where they're easy to see, and away from fences and other things that cats and squirrels can jump on.

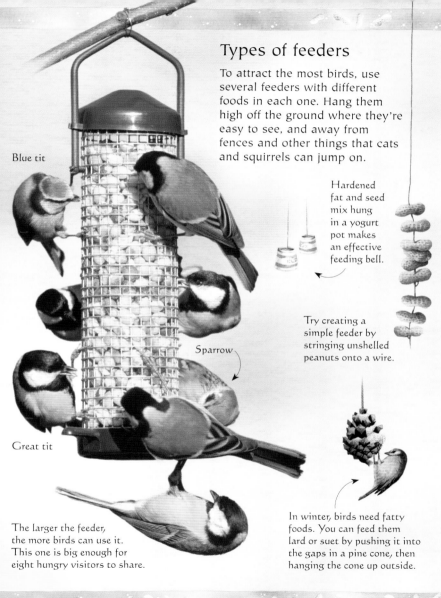

Blue tit

Hardened fat and seed mix hung in a yogurt pot makes an effective feeding bell.

Sparrow

Try creating a simple feeder by stringing unshelled peanuts onto a wire.

Great tit

The larger the feeder, the more birds can use it. This one is big enough for eight hungry visitors to share.

In winter, birds need fatty foods. You can feed them lard or suet by pushing it into the gaps in a pine cone, then hanging the cone up outside.

What to offer

Feeding birds can be as simple as scattering crumbs on a branch or pushing lumps of cheese into the cracks of a tree trunk. Bird feeders can be filled with plain sunflower seeds and unsalted peanuts, or you can buy pre-mixed bird food from a shop.

Mixture of nuts, grains and seeds

Freeze-dried mealworms

Peanuts

Pumpkin seeds

Make a food garland

You will need:

✿ long piece of thread ✿ darning needle
✿ big pieces of popped popcorn

Pull the needle a little way along the folded thread.

1. Make a loop in the middle of the thread and pass it through the hole in the needle.

2. Carefully push the needle through the popcorn, pulling each piece along the thread.

3. Pull the thread out of the needle. Tie knots at both ends. Wind the garland tightly around a branch.

Make a bird cake

For the cake mixture, use two cupfuls of these ingredients in any combination:

- breadcrumbs
- biscuit crumbs
- peanuts
- cooked oatmeal
- currants
- chopped apple
- sunflower seeds
- raisins
- muesli

You will also need:

- cupful of solid fat
- wooden spoon
- mixing bowl
- saucepan

1. Using the spoon, mix all of your ingredients except the fat in the bowl.

2. In the saucepan, melt the fat on a low heat. Slowly pour it over the mixture. Leave it to set.

3. When the cake is cold, turn it out. Put it outside on a raised platform, such as a bird table.

Tiny seeds can make a tasty treat for birds of all sizes, from large pigeons to little sparrows, like these.

Bird detective

Sometimes you might not see all the birds that live nearby,
but you can keep an eye out for clues that tell you where
they've been and even what they've been eating.

Finding feathers

In summer, many birds grow new feathers to
replace their old, worn ones. You can find
discarded feathers in spots where birds
roost or eat. Make sure you wash
your hands after touching them.

Curlew
feather

Magpie
feather

Pheasant
feather

To identify the feathers you find,
you can try to match them with
the colours and markings of
birds in a field guide.

Mallard
feather

Jay feather

Barn owl
feather

Footprints with one long
toe behind three front toes
belong to birds that perch.

Tracking footprints

A bird's footprints are often hard to
spot, as birds don't spend much time
on the ground and, when there, they
tread lightly. If you find a bird's tracks,
look for clues to where it lives and
how it moves. Hopping birds have
paired tracks, while walking birds'
prints lie one in front of the other.

A wading bird's
tracks show long,
spreading toes.

Ducks leave
webbed tracks
on muddy banks.

Many birds
that swim have
webbed prints.

Bird pellets

Some birds swallow their food whole, then cough up pellets of the parts they can't digest. These parcels can be made up of fur, bones, feathers or insect parts. If you come across a pellet, you can look what's inside.

Gulls forage on rubbish dumps so, as well as bits of food, there might be some other odds and ends in their pellets.

Fish bone

Scrap of foil

Looking inside a pellet

Water with a few drops of disinfectant

Wash your hands when you've finished.

1. Soak the pellet for an hour. Put it on an old newspaper. Use cocktail sticks to prise it apart.

2. Using a pair of tweezers, pick out the hard parts, such as teeth and bones.

3. Clean the hard bits with a dry paint brush and look at them with a magnifying glass.

Signs of feeding

You can find out what food the birds in your area eat by looking for signs of pecking on nuts, cones, fruits and plants.

Like this fieldfare, many birds can't finish a big piece of food in one go, and will often leave it half-eaten.

Birds leave peck marks in nuts.

Other animals, such as rodents, might leave teeth marks.

Town and city birds

Birds live in all kinds of places, even those built specifically for people. In towns and cities all over the world, you'll find birds thriving amidst the buildings, bustle and traffic.

Tame birds

It's easy to watch birds that live in town and city centres, as they're not difficult to find and are used to being around people. They're often reasonably tame, but it's safest not to touch them.

Unruffled by passing traffic and pedestrians, a feral pigeon takes a refreshing drink from a public fountain.

Pigeons often fly over built-up areas in huge groups.

Soaring over busy streets, gulls scout for food scraps.

Noisy flocks of chattering starlings gather on rooftops.

City visitors

Some country birds visit urban regions every winter, to take advantage of the food and warmth that built-up areas provide.

In winter, skylarks fly from the open countryside to city parks and wasteground.

City songs

The noise of the city can often drown out birds' songs. To make themselves heard, some city birds sing at a higher pitch than their country cousins. You can also hear some birds singing at night.

City great tits sing higher melodies than country great tits.

As night falls, street lights turn on, prompting robins to burst into song.

On your doorstep

For birds that live near people's homes, finding food can be as simple as turning up on their human neighbours' doorsteps.

Blue tits occasionally peck holes in milk bottle tops to sip the milk inside.

The radiators of parked cars make good feeding grounds for insect-eating house sparrows.

White storks sometimes construct their huge nests in chimneys.

Building sites

Some of the best places to see urban birds' nests are in parks and on wasteground. Look out for them nestled in trees and bushes, or sitting by ponds and lakes. You might spot them in more built-up areas, too.

Undisturbed junkyards and dumping grounds are full of nooks and crannies where city birds, like this robin, can build their nests.

In the country

From grassy fields to boggy marshes, the countryside offers a wide range of habitats for birds. You'll spot different kinds of birds in each area.

Woods and forests

Places where there are a lot of trees make good nesting sites for birds. A tree's fruits, nuts, seeds and even their insect inhabitants also provide birds with an array of tasty treats.

Jays collect acorns from oak trees, bury them, then dig them up later when they need food.

Hungry crossbills find seeds by prising open cones that grow on pine trees.

If you find a hole surrounded by mud in a tree, it may be a nuthatch's nesting hole.

Treecreepers crawl up tree trunks, devouring insects.

Fields and hedges

Hedgerows, fields and meadows are stocked full of food for birds. They feast on plants and small animals in hedges and amongst crops, and gobble up insects that buzz around farm animals, too.

Pheasants nest and feed in fields.

Heathland birds

In summer, it may seem as if heaths are only inhabited by plant life, but they're also teeming with insects, so attract many insect-eating birds. As there aren't many trees around, birds tend to nest in or under bushes.

Stonechats and linnets nest in thick gorse bushes on heaths.

Stonechat

Linnets

Boggy marshes

Marshes are open areas of grass and reeds, which are wet for most of the time. Many marsh birds live close to the ground, so are difficult to spot, but you might see some small birds perched on top of the rustling reeds.

Reed warblers sometimes rest on reedtops, but prefer to stay hidden further down.

Ponds and streams

Still or slow-flowing water attracts lots of different types of birds. Some spend most of their lives in and around the water, while others just visit to have a drink or take a dip.

This tufted duck is "upending" to grab prey beneath the surface.

Kingfishers grab fish from the water, then fly to a perch with the fish in their beaks.

Tufted duck right way up

A shoveler duck sieves food from the water with its bill.

Moorhens spend as much time on land as they do in the water.

Harsh environments

High up on bleak moors and misty mountains, there's very little food or shelter for birds. Some of the world's toughest birds live in these challenging habitats.

High and low

Barren landscapes are good places to look for birds of prey. In mountains, they soar high on strong winds and nest on towering, rocky ledges. On moors, they stay close to the ground, nesting in heather and bracken, and flying low to look for small animals to eat.

Golden eagles prey on hares and other small mountain mammals.

Short-eared owls hunt on moors during the day.

Hen harriers nest amongst moorland plants.

Perching motionless, a merlin looks out over the moors, watching for prey.

Short-toed eagles snap up snakes that slither through long, moorland grass.

Hidden away

Moors and mountains are home to some types of game birds, which are hunted by birds of prey and by people, too. With so many enemies, game birds have to be masters of disguise, spending a lot of time crouched in bushes and thick patches of undergrowth.

Ptarmigans nest hidden among rocks or bushes.

To help it hide in all seasons, a willow grouse's feathers change from brown in summer to white in winter.

Unfussy eaters

As there isn't much food in their moorland habitats, ravens eat almost anything. They mainly feed on dead animals, even pecking out the eyeballs. If there aren't any animals or insects around, they'll resort to eating grass.

Ravens tear meat with their strong, hooked beaks.

Going for a dip

Rivers and streams that run down mountains usually flow very rapidly. Most birds don't go near these fierce waters, but you might spot a few small birds dipping their beaks in from a safe perching place.

Dippers swim, dive, and walk along the bottom of fast-flowing streams in search of food.

Grey wagtails stand on rocks to snatch water insects from rapids.

Birds in danger

Over the years, many birds have been harmed by people, both accidentally and deliberately. Today, there are laws to protect birds, but they still have man-made dangers to face.

Altering habitats

When habitats, such as fields or woods, are farmed intensively or cleared for construction, birds can find themselves homeless. Those that can't adapt to living in other areas begin to die out.

The number of black-tailed godwits declines when their wetland breeding grounds are drained for farming.

This photograph may be the closest you'll come to a tree sparrow. This species has been dying out, as an increasing use of pesticides has made it harder for them to find insects to eat.

Corn buntings die out when the weeds they feed on are removed to make space for crops.

Dangerous waters

Rubbish, waste chemicals and oil are sometimes spilled or even illegally dumped on beaches and into rivers and oceans, harming water birds.

Plastic rings that used to hold cans together can strangle birds.

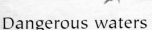

It's helpful to cut up the rings, and put them in a recycling bin.

Toxic chemicals

For birds of prey, there's a risk that the animals they eat could have fed on plants sprayed with various chemical pesticides and weed killers. These chemicals can build up in the bird's body and poison it.

In the 1950s and 60s, hundreds of peregrine falcons perished when a pesticide called DDT was sprayed on crops. DDT is now banned.

Red kites are harmed by feeding on rodents that have been poisoned as pests.

Hunting

Some local populations of game birds have been hunted to alarmingly low levels. Many countries now have restrictions on the number of birds that can be shot for sport.

Red-legged partridge

In some European countries, legal and illegal hunting has drastically reduced the red-legged partridge and capercaillie populations.

Capercaillie

Trapping and collecting

Trappers catch wild songbirds illegally and sell them as pets. Collectors also steal birds' eggs. The rarer the bird, the more its eggs are sought after.

Trappers target songbirds, such as linnets, to be sold as cage birds.

Protecting birds

Many organizations look after birds, giving them safe places to feed and nest. You can help birds by joining a bird protection group or simply by caring for the birds in your area.

Managing the land

If a bird species is dying out, conservation organizations work with landowners, advising them on how to manage their land in ways that will help these threatened birds.

Farmers are helped to make wet meadows on their land, providing feeding and nesting sites for birds, such as lapwings.

Protected places

Some governments, charities and private landowners have set aside land for wildlife to live on, where building and hunting is very tightly restricted. These nature reserves can range from a few fields to vast national parks.

Stretches of water on nature reserves can attract many varieties of ducks, geese and other freshwater birds.

You might spot a colourful kingfisher, like this one, perched beside a quiet backwater on a nature reserve.

Shelduck

Goldeneye

Brent goose

Finding a nest

Discovering a bird's nest can be very exciting, but it's important not to touch it. If a bird senses that its nest has been disturbed, it may abandon it as well as any eggs inside it.

In many countries, it's illegal to move a nest, even if it's on the side of a house, like this house martin's nest.

Although this song thrush's nest is empty, the bird could return to it when it's ready to lay eggs again.

Finding baby birds

A chick sitting on the ground by itself may look as if it needs rescuing, but its parents are likely to be close by, watching over it. If a chick has fallen out of its nest and can't get back, you can look for the nest nearby and gently put it inside.

Blackbird chick

Young robin

Young lapwing

A featherless chick on the ground is likely to have fallen out of its nest.

Young birds covered in down feathers are probably old enough to look after themselves.

Safe haven

Gardens are often the main source of food for local birds but, even here, they might face dangers. People can make gardens safe for birds by keeping them free from chemical pest killers and by putting quick-release bell collars on their cats, so birds can hear them coming.

Myths and legends

In ancient times, birds were seen as symbols of power and religious figures. Today, birds still play an important role in the culture and religion of people all over the world.

Power and glory

Throughout history, the leaders of nations have used birds as symbols of authority and freedom. Today, birds still appear on many flags and coats of arms.

The bird of paradise is the national emblem of Papua New Guinea and it features on the country's flag.

Roman soldiers were led into battle by a standard-bearer, whose job it was to hold up a statue of an eagle.

Curious creatures

Many ancient cultures have legends of mythical birds with magical abilities. One such bird is the phoenix, which dies in a burst of flames, only to be reborn, as a new phoenix rises from the ashes.

Phoenixes appear in legends from Egypt, Greece and China. The stories vary, but many describe the bird as having flaming wings and a tail of fire.

Sacred symbols

Stories from many religions link birds with higher powers, such as gods or goddesses. Birds were seen as suitable symbols due to their grace and strength but, most of all, because of their superhuman ability to fly.

Hundreds of years ago, the Aztec peoples of Central America regarded quetzal birds as symbols of their god of the air and sky.

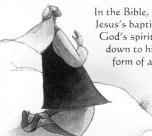

In the Bible, the story of Jesus's baptism tells of God's spirit coming down to him in the form of a dove.

The Ancient Greeks believed that Athena, their goddess of wisdom, could turn herself into an owl.

Soul carriers

Many legends tell of birds carrying people's souls. There are tales of sea birds delivering the souls of dead sailors to heaven, of doves taking lovers' souls to their sweethearts, and even of souls looking like birds with human heads.

It was considered bad luck to kill these sea birds, as people thought they carried the souls of drowned sailors.

Albatross

Ancient Egyptians believed they had bird-like souls which flew from their bodies when they died.

Black-headed gull

Amazing but true

Biggest...
Ostriches are both the tallest and the heaviest birds. They reach a height of up to 2.5m (8ft) tall and a weight of 156.5kg (350lbs).

Despite being the heaviest birds, ostriches are also the fastest runners, reaching speeds of up to 97kph (60mph).

...and smallest
The tiniest birds are bee hummingbirds. They're even smaller than bumblebees and weigh just 1.6g (0.06oz).

Widest wingspan
When fully stretched, the wings of a wandering albatross measure about 3.5m (11½ ft) from tip to tip, the same as two men lying end to end.

Wandering albatross

Chatterboxes
African grey parrots can be taught to say around 800 words. They can learn to recite short poems, and even sing lyrics.

As well as words, African grey parrots can mimic other noises, such as ringing doorbells and pinging microwaves.

Bumper beaks
Australian pelicans have the longest beaks. They can grow up to 45cm (18in) long, which is about the length of a computer keyboard.

Most feathers
Tundra swans (also called North American whistling swans) are covered with over 25,000 feathers.

Frequent flappers

Hummingbirds usually flap their wings 40-80 times a second. When a male is trying to impress a female, it increases its flapping to 200 times a second.

A ruby-throated hummingbird flaps about 80 times a second as it hovers.

Treetop mansions

Bald eagles build nests that are around 3m (9½ft) wide and 6m (20ft) deep. That's big enough to fit several people inside.

Breathtaking divers

Emperor penguins can stay under water for longer than any other bird, diving for up to 18 minutes in one breath.

Emperor penguins

Counting chickens

Of the 100,000 million birds in the world, around 3,000 million are domestic chickens.

Fast movers

The speediest swimmers are gentoo penguins. They can zip along at speeds of up to 27kph (17mph).

Its torpedo-shaped body helps this gentoo penguin reach its top speeds when swimming under water.

Mini-nests

The smallest nests are built by vervain hummingbirds. At just 1.5cm (½ in) across, the nests are about the width of a person's thumbnail.

Vervain hummingbird eggs are just 1cm (¹/₃in) long.

Hyacinth macaw

Tough bills

Hyacinth macaws – the world's largest parrots – have beaks that are so strong they can crack coconuts and snap metal bars in two.

Dazzling display

When showing off to a female, a male Temminck's tragopan raises two soft horns on its head and exposes a bright blue and red flap of skin on its chest.

Temminck's tragopan

Child protection

Robins only grow red feathers after they are a few months old. Young robins are speckled. This lets adult birds know not to attack them in disputes over territory.

Snowy sounds

A snowy owl has such sharp hearing that it can pick up sounds made by prey buried up to 25cm (10in) under snow.

Snowy owl

Enormous eggs
Ostriches lay the biggest eggs. They're about 18cm (7in) long and 14cm (5½in) wide, which is bigger than this book.

In the pink
The rosy colouring in a flamingo's feathers comes from the coloured chemicals called carotenoids in the tiny shrimps that they feed on. If they don't eat the shrimps, their feathers turn pale.

Lammergeiers live on crags in high mountains.

Flamingos use their beaks to filter shrimps from the water.

Quite a mouthful
The lower half of a pelican's bill can stretch to hold up to 11 litres (3 gallons) of water, which is many times more than its stomach can hold.

Pelican

Dead drop
Lammergeiers feed on tortoises by lifting them in their huge claws, flying high into the air, then dropping them onto the rocks below to crack them open.

Adding up the numbers
Of all the world's wild birds, red-billed Queleas have the highest population. There are around 1,500 million of them, all living in Africa.

Furthest travellers
Every year, sooty shearwaters migrate around 74,000km (46,000 miles). They fly in a figure-of-eight pattern around the Pacific Ocean from California, to Japan, to New Zealand, and back again.

Trees

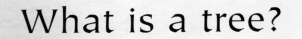

What is a tree?

Trees are the Earth's ancient giants. They can grow bigger than any other plant and live longer than any animal.

High and mighty

Most trees have one trunk, a thick stem that rises some way above the ground before branching into twiggy boughs. Fully grown, trees are usually at least 6m (20ft) tall, and many grow several times higher.

With its sturdy wooden trunk, this Douglas fir tree may grow to 60m (200ft).

Scots pines like these were overlooking this valley before the first people settled there.

Tree or shrub?

Woody plants under 6m (20ft), with several stems, are known as shrubs. Some plants that are trees in the wild can be shrubs if kept trimmed.

A clipped Leyland cypress makes a neat bush; uncut, it can grow into a 40m (130ft) monster.

Long lives

For many plants, life is over in a few short months, but a tree's stiff trunk and tough bark let it survive year after year. Some trees live for many centuries.

Giant sequoias can live for over 3,000 years.

The older a tree, the greater the range of living things it supports.

Protecting life

Trees provide shelter for thousands of animal and plant species, and their leaves, fruits and seeds are food for many more. Their roots hold soil in place, while their leaves make oxygen gas that people and animals need to breathe. Without trees, little could survive.

Fieldfares feast on rowan berries.

Treecreepers spiral up tree trunks, hunting for insects.

Nut weevils lay their eggs in acorns.

Toadstools often appear at the foot of trees.

Butterflies feed on fallen fruit.

Types of tree

There are over 80,000 kinds of tree in the world. Whether they grow in well-kept parks or tangled forests, most of them belong to one of two groups: conifers and broadleaves.

Needles and scales

Conifers have tough little leaves shaped like needles or scales. They are usually evergreen, which means they stay on the tree all year, only falling off when new leaves grow. Most young conifers are rocket-shaped, with straight trunks.

Shore pine needles

Giant sequoia scales

Sitka spruces grow very tall and straight.

Cone bearers

Conifers were named because their seeds grow in woody cones (the word "conifer" means "cone-bearer"). The seeds lie tucked safely in between the scales of the cones until they're ripe and ready to be released.

This Scots pine cone has opened to allow its ripe seeds to scatter.

Douglas fir cone

Broadleaf trees

Broadleaves have bigger, wider leaves than conifers, with more varied shapes. Many trees are deciduous, losing their leaves each autumn. Their trunks often divide into several main branches, making them bushier than conifers. Broadleaves bear a wide variety of fruits, ranging from rosy apples to wizened walnuts.

Sweet chestnut seeds are cased inside prickly fruits.

London plane leaves have ragged edges. Their fruits are round and bristly.

Elder trees bear bunches of purplish-black berries.

Broadleaves are often not as symmetrical as conifer trees.

Sweet chestnut

Common pear

Bobble fruit

Palm trees

Palm trees grow mainly in hot and steamy parts of the world known as the tropics. They're not related to conifers or broadleaves, but to lilies and grasses, and grow very differently from other trees.

Some palm leaves fan out like giant hands.

Palm trunks get taller but not wider each year, and most have no branches.

Lush leaves

A tree's leaves act like solar panels, soaking up energy from the Sun. They're also food factories, producing the nourishment trees need to grow.

Green power

Leaves get their green colour from a chemical called chlorophyll. This uses sunlight energy to join carbon dioxide gas from the air with water from the soil. The result is a sugary sap which trees use as food.

Some leaves also contain dark-coloured chemicals that hide chlorophyll, so the leaves don't look green, even in spring.

Copper beech

A few leaf types are only green in patches. They can't make as much food so they grow more slowly.

Golden holly

Spread out like this, these lime leaves can absorb as much light as possible.

In the pipeline

Look closely at a leaf, and you'll see a network of fine veins. These pipe watery sap up from the roots, and send sugary sap from the leaves around the tree.

Leaf shapes

Leaves come in many shapes and sizes, whether oval or pointed, long and skinny or broad and raggedy. Even on a single tree, no two leaves are exactly alike.

Lobed leaves, like this white poplar, have wiggly outlines.

A leaf from lower down on the same tree has smaller lobes.

Whitebeam leaves have jagged edges.

The leaves of white willow trees are long and slender.

Compound leaves, like this ash, are made up of several smaller leaves, called leaflets.

Heart-shaped lime leaves have long "drip-tips" so water can run off easily.

Each horse chestnut leaf has leaflets that splay out from a central point.

Conifer leaves

From a distance, conifer trees may look similar, but a closer look will soon show you that their needles and scales grow in very different ways.

Cedar needles grow mainly in rosettes.

Cypresses have tiny scales.

Pine needles grow in bunches.

Fir needles grow all along the twig.

Root and branch

A tree's branches spread widely
as it reaches for sunlight. Below the ground,
hidden from view, its roots often spread wider still.

Putting down roots

Roots anchor a tree firmly in the earth,
keeping it upright on windy days. Even
more importantly, they grow down into
the soil, soaking up water and minerals.
Roots also store a tree's winter food.

Most of a tree's
roots spread out
sideways, keeping
the trunk stable.

Piping up

Apart from lifting the leaves nearer
to energizing sunlight, the trunk's
main role is to act as a water pipe.
It channels watery sap, filled with
health-giving minerals, from the
roots up into the leaves.

Thick tree roots divide
into ever finer ones.

Thirsty work

Leaves take in air through minute
holes in their undersides. As this
happens, the leaves are dried out
by sun and wind. To replace the
moisture, a constant supply
of watery sap is drawn
up from the roots.

Air holes
(25x life
size)

Underside

The root tips are covered
in microscopic hairs which
soak up water from the soil.

A root may have to
grow around stones
or other obstacles.

Branching out

Unlike animals, trees don't stretch out as they grow, but only lengthen from the tips of their branches. Unless it breaks off, a side branch will always be the same height from the ground, no matter how thick it becomes.

A young tree's side branches begin to grow.

As the trunk grows wider and taller, the branches grow thicker and longer.

Twiggy branches once grew low on this trunk. As the tree grew, the branches withered in its shade, or were eaten by passing animals.

Pine branches

The branches of many pine trees grow in evenly spaced whorls that you may see on its trunk. A new set of branches grows each year, so counting the whorls can give you a good idea of how old a tree is.

The number of branch whorls, and scars left by branches, on the trunk of this Corsican pine shows it's about eight years old.

Sturdy trunks

Compared with rustling leaves or swaying branches, a tree trunk may not attract a second glance. But there's more to these woody pillars than meets the eye.

Dead and alive

Every year, a trunk gets fatter as new wood grows behind the bark. This sapwood is full of tiny tubes that carry watery sap from the roots to the leaves. As the years pass, the older tubes harden and die, forming a supportive core of heartwood.

— Bark

— Heartwood

— Sapwood

If a tree makes more food than it needs, the extra is stored in these pale rays.

Count the rings

Every tree stump tells a story. The number of rings shows how old a tree was when it was cut down. Wide rings record good growth years, with plenty of light and food. Narrow rings show years of drought or overcrowding.

By counting its rings you can see this tree was about 40 years old when it was felled.

Darker, slow-growing summer wood

Annual rings, magnified

Lighter, fast-growing spring wood

Like a trunk, branches and twigs grow in rings.

Bark

Bark is like a protective skin, keeping the living wood from drying out, being damaged, or freezing. It's made up of a waterproof outer layer on top of a corky under-bark. Tubes inside the bark carry sugary sap from the leaves around the tree.

Cork oaks grow in southern Europe. They have very thick bark, which is harvested to make bottle stoppers.

Cork

Cracking up

Bark is dead, so it can't grow or stretch. Instead, as the tree gets wider, it cracks, flakes or peels off, revealing the newer bark beneath. Some trees can be recognized just by the texture of their bark.

Beech bark crumbles off in tiny chips.

Sitka spruce bark breaks off in big flakes.

Sycamore bark falls off in large pieces.

Silver birch bark peels away in strips.

Paper birches, like this, are named because of their peeling, parchment-like bark.

A tree is born

Most trees grow from seeds. All winter, a seed lies in the
cool earth. Inside it, the beginnings of a baby tree await
the gentle warmth of the weak spring sunshine.

Springing up

In spring, the seed takes in water, and swells up. Its
first root burrows into the soil, and a slender shoot
pushes upwards. Seed leaves open to receive light,
and a tender bud appears.

Sycamore seed

Root

Bud

Roots grow.

The little root grows
down, reaching the water
and minerals it needs.

Seed leaves are a different
shape from later leaves. A
bud nestles between them.

One day,
this fragile
seedling may
be a mighty
oak tree.

Summer seedlings

In summer, the bud opens and the true leaves
of the young tree, or seedling, unfold. A new
bud forms at the base of each leaf.

True leaves unfold.

No longer needed,
the seed leaves
wither and die.

The acorn shell
rots away as the
young tree grows.

Autumn and winter

When autumn comes, the leaves die and fall off, leaving scars on the stem. Throughout the winter, the "leader" bud, at the tip of the shoot, is protected by leaf-like bud scales.

Leader bud grows into a main shoot.

Side buds grow into side shoots.

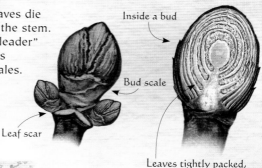

Inside a bud

Bud scale

Leaf scar

Leaves tightly packed, like a Brussels sprout

Growing up

In a seedling's second spring, its buds open and the bud scales fall off, leaving scars. Through spring and summer, the buds unfurl their new leaves for that year, and the shoots grow longer. This cycle of growth will carry on throughout its life.

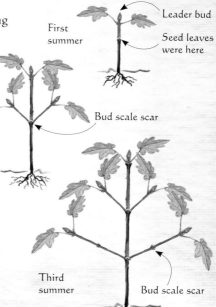

First summer

Leader bud

Seed leaves were here

Bud scale scar

Second summer

Suckers

Sometimes, new trees are made without seeds, by putting up new shoots from their roots. These are called suckers.

Western balsam poplar often spreads using sucker roots.

Third summer

Bud scale scar

Taking shape

Different tree types have distinctive shapes. There's often variation between individual trees, too, as they grow reacting to their surroundings.

At a glance

Some trees can be recognized just by their outlines, or the way their branches are arranged. You can see this best in winter, when many trees are leafless.

This Norway spruce's cone-like shape is typical of young conifers.

Scots pine has a bare trunk.

Ashes grow tall and very open at the top.

Weeping willow branches droop gracefully down.

Lombardy poplars are elegant trees with tightly packed, upright branches.

Living room

The shape of a developing tree is strongly influenced by the number of other trees growing nearby.

English oaks in open spaces grow into a rounded shape.

In a crowded forest, oaks grow taller and thinner as they fight for light.

Sun, rain and snow

Local climates around the world affect both the type of trees suited to growing there, and the shape of particular trees.

Western hemlock grows in the snowy mountains of North America. Its short, bendy branches slope down so that snow slides off.

This stone pine grows in Italy. Its shallow, umbrella shape lets hot, drying winds slip easily past.

Trees in hot, wet rainforests grow all year round, shooting up on skinny trunks as they compete for sunlight.

Wind sculpture

Trees growing by the coast or on hillsides are often shaped by the wind. They can take the most fantastic forms as they struggle to survive the gusts and gales.

The constant buffeting of salty sea storms has forced this juniper to grow branches on its more sheltered side.

Spring blooms

As spring arrives, tree buds burst open, unfolding their new leaves and flowers. Flowers that grow on trees, especially fruit trees, are often known as blossoms.

Flower power

This splendid magnolia bloom is one of the largest flowers of any tree.

Some tree flowers are big and showy; others are so small they hardly seem like flowers at all. However they look, they all have a vital job: producing seeds to make new trees.

Elm flowers are tiny red specks.

Elder trees have clusters of little white flowers.

Male and female

Blossoms are male or female, or have male and female parts in a single flower. To make seeds, the females must first be sprinkled with pollen, a powder made by the males. This is known as pollination.

Beech trees have both male and female flowers.

Female

Male

Male

Female

Rowan flowers have male and female parts.

On the breeze

Trees can't travel around, so they need help to spread their pollen. Some use the wind to carry it. They tend to have clusters of tiny flowers with no petals.

Larch has pink-tipped female flowers that grow on its upper branches...

...Pollen drifts upwards from yellow male flowers on the lower branches.

Male and female crack willow flowers grow on separate trees.

Like many wind-pollinated trees, crack willows have fuzzy flower clusters called catkins.

The wind shakes out the pollen.

Male

Female

Hired help

Some trees use insects to carry their pollen. They attract them with fragrant-petalled flowers, and a sweet liquid called nectar. As the bees sip the nectar, they become coated with pollen, which rubs off onto the next flowers they then visit.

This bee is carrying pollen in "baskets" on its legs.

Bees visit apple blossom in the afternoon, when the nectar is at its richest.

Bees can tell which horse chestnut flowers are making nectar by their yellow marks.

Fruit and seeds

If you think of fruit, the first things that spring to mind are often colour, shape and taste. But to a tree, the most important part is the seed inside.

From flowers to fruit

After a flower is pollinated, its petals drop off, and it develops into a fruit. The fruit's job is to keep its seeds safe inside until they're ripe, and then to get them far enough away from the tree to grow. This is so new trees don't have to compete with their parent for space, light and water.

Section of rowan berry, showing seeds

Pear

Rowan berries

Some fruits, such as apples, pears and rowan berries, hold their seeds in a fleshy core.

Mulberries are made up of berry-like parts, each with its own seed.

This is the remains of the flower.

Fruits such as plums and cherries have a single, hard seed.

Apple

Figs are unusual fruits: the flowers grow inside them, developing into hundreds of seeds.

Cherry

Plum

Juicy fruit

Fruit are often tasty to encourage animals to eat them and carry them away inside their bodies. The seeds later pop out in their droppings, so wherever they land, they have a little dollop of fertilizer to boost their growth.

Bullfinches eat elderberries in autumn.

Holly berries are a winter treat for woodmice.

In summer, wasps feast upon the sweet, gloopy goodness of fallen plums.

Tough nuts

Nuts are a type of dry fruit made up of a hard shell, protecting a large seed. They are packed with nourishment, and relished by animals.

Horse chestnuts, or conkers, are eaten by deer and cattle.

Walnuts have a large seed in a thin, woody shell.

If this squirrel buries its nut to eat when food is scarce but then forgets about it, the nut may sprout into a new tree.

Helicopter ride

Some trees have dry, papery fruit shaped like wings. As the wind catches them, they twirl away, carrying their seeds far and wide. Other fruits fall apart, releasing seeds with feathery parachutes that drift along on the breeze.

These maple "keys" hang on the tree until late summer, when they fall and flutter away.

Sycamore keys have two wings.

Ash keys have a single wing.

Fluffy willow catkins fall apart, releasing their seeds.

Feathery tufts keep willow seeds aloft.

Elm seeds are enclosed in papery wings.

Plane tree bobble fruits break up in the wind.

Bobble fruit seeds

Cones

On conifer trees the female flowers grow into woody cones with tough scales that protect their seeds. The scales only open to release the seeds when the weather is warm and dry.

A Scots pine cone releasing its seeds

These seeds are spread by the wind.

Birds such as this crossbill prise open cones to eat their seeds.

Norway spruce cones

Cones aren't always cone-shaped. These unripe cypress cones look more like large, dried peas.

The cones of a stone pine take three years to ripen. People harvest their edible seeds, which are known as pine nuts.

Junipers and yews have small, fleshy cones that look like berries.

Atlas cedar cones are egg-shaped. They slowly fall apart on the branch, and their winged seeds are blown away.

Yew

Seed

Juniper

Seed

Open and shut

You can see for yourself how a cone opens in dry weather, by placing a closed one near a radiator. Its scales will slowly open as it dries out.

In cold, damp weather a cone stays shut.

When the weather is warm and dry, its scales unfold.

Autumn glory

Of all seasons, autumn is often the most spectacular.
As fruit ripens on their branches, many trees put on a
display of fiery crimsons and oranges, golds and browns.

Goodbye to greenery

Silver maple

Winter's freezing weather is dangerous for
soft, vulnerable leaves, and its short days
make it hard for them to absorb sunlight.
Deciduous trees prepare for this testing
time by losing their leaves in autumn.

The chemical that is turning these
horse chestnut leaves yellow
is also found in bananas.

As this leaf loses
its green chlorophyll
and dries out, hidden
colours are revealed.

The leaf dies and is
blown off, leaving
behind a scar, and
a bud with next
year's leaves.

All fall down

The leaves of most deciduous trees fall over a few weeks. Some, such as young beeches, keep dead leaves on their lower parts all winter, until they are replaced by new ones in spring.

Horse chestnut leaves fall as early as September.

Trees lose their leaves at different times.

Oak leaves may drop as late as November.

Rowan

Copper beech

A ginkgo's leaves may all fall off in one day.

Red oak

Make a leaf album

Autumn is the best time of year to collect fallen leaves. See how many different types you can find – a field guide will help you identify them. If you like, you could stick them into an album.

A field guide will help you to identify the leaves you find.

1. Press some clean, dry leaves between sheets of blotting paper, weighed down by heavy books.

2. Wait a few weeks, then stick the pressed leaves into a scrapbook with tape.

Trees in winter

Winter is a challenging time for many trees.
While some are cloaked with leaves that can endure
the cold, others stand naked to survive the season.

Wax jackets

Evergreen leaves are specially
designed to withstand wintry
weather. A waxy coating
keeps them from freezing
in the frosty air.
The shape of the
leaves helps them
survive, too.

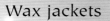

Unlike most conifer
leaves, larch needles
aren't waxy, so the trees
shed them in autumn.

Holly leaves are broad
and flat, but their thick
waterproof covering
protects them.

Long, thin Scots pine
needles lose water far
less easily than wider,
flatter leaves.

Snowflakes can't pile
up on these narrow
pine needles, so even a
heavy snowfall leaves
only a light sprinkling.

Winter buds

Without their leaves, a tree's buds and overall shapes are easier to see. A field guide will help you to identify them. Here are a few examples you could look out for:

Beech

Beech buds are brown and spiky.

Sycamore

Sycamores have large, green buds with dark-edged scales.

Sweet chestnut

Sweet chestnut has knobbly twigs and big, reddish buds.

Grow your own

If you want to watch buds open before spring, you could take a twig cutting and keep it indoors. Do ask permission from the tree's owner first.

Buds

Sturdy scissors

1. Find a tree with plump buds and snip off a few 25cm (10in) twigs. Goat willow works well.

2. Put the cuttings in a jam jar of water and leave it in a warm, sunny place indoors.

3. Keep the water topped up. In a few weeks, the buds will start to open.

Growing old

Trees may live for hundreds or thousands of years. As their trunks widen each growing season, trees can be extremely fat by the time they reach old age.

Looks can deceive

Some trees may not be the age they seem because they grow much more quickly or slowly than others. Their life span also affects when they're considered to be old.

These trees all have trunks 3m (9¼ft) around.

At 120 years, this beech is middle aged.

Cedars of Lebanon grow rapidly, for trees. This one could be just 45.

Yews grow very slowly. This one is 235, but is still in its infancy.

Signs of ageing

Apart from their size, old trees often look gnarled. Most show a history of damage, such as holes, dead branches or sap oozing out of a crack in the bark.

Fungi such as this giant polypore often grow on old trees.

Ivy

Fern

Lichen

Old trees are often festooned with ferns, lichen, ivy and other climbing plants.

Animal holes are a common sign of age in trees.

Estimating age

In open spaces, most trunks widen by about 2.5cm
(1in) every year (half that in forests). This means,
for example, that a lone oak whose trunk measures
2.5m (8½ft) around could be 100 years old.

Stagheads

Big, old trees sometimes outgrow the
water supply their roots can provide.
Their heaviest branches may then
die and break off, giving them
an antler-like "staghead" look.

Some old trees
lose branches
to save water.

Not dead yet

Trees that appear to be dead
may still be surviving. Even
when its heartwood has
completely rotted away,
a tree can still grow new
leaves every year.

This oak is over 1,000 years
old, and completely hollow.
Amazingly, dinner parties
for 20 people are said to
have been held inside it.

Death and afterlife

Even a tree that lasts for a thousand years dies eventually. But its story does not end there, as it goes on to support the lives of many other things.

A time to die

With its tough-looking bark, a tree may seem invincible, but even a small injury can leave it open to attack from fungi and insects, leading to deadly disease. This may finish off a tree long before its time.

Sawn branch

Trees can't easily heal injuries.

Three years later

They slowly grow new bark to seal them off.

Six years later

This takes them a very long time.

Scale insects cling to bark like limpet shells. They infest trees, sucking out their sap.

Scale insects

Elm bark beetles tunnel under bark to lay their eggs. As they do so, they spread fungi which causes Dutch elm disease.

Elm bark beetle

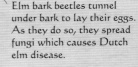

English elm

Some fungi, such as this dryad's saddle, invade a tree through a wound and grow, causing decay that rots its heartwood.

Most of the English elms in Britain were killed by Dutch elm disease in the 1960s.

Dead good

A third of woodland creatures rely on dead wood for food or a place to live, so dead trees and fallen logs are vital to their survival.

Pipistrelle bat

Bats rest in tree holes during the day.

Long-eared bat

Weasels live in hollow logs or holes in dead trees.

Hollow trees make daytime hideaways for night birds such as this barn owl.

Log cabin

Creepy-crawlies are very much at home in a rotting log. Next time you pass one, look closely to see what has moved in.

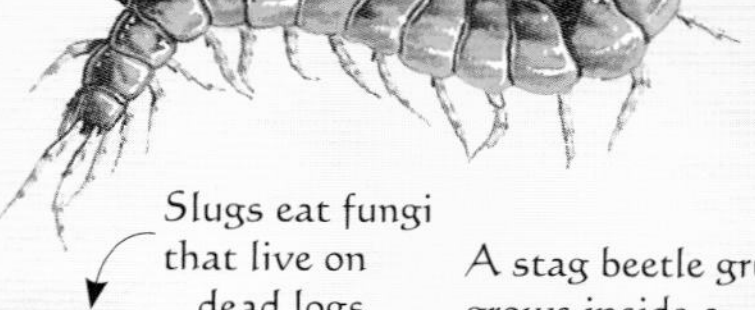

Centipedes live under dead bark, scuttling out at night to hunt small insects.

Stag beetles lay their eggs in crumbling wood in summer.

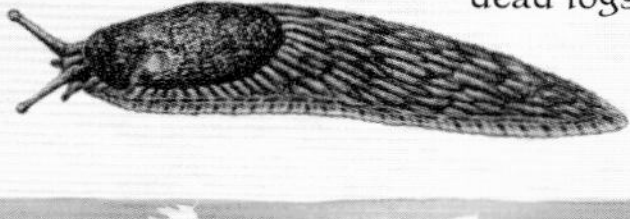

Decaying wood is food for a woodlouse.

Slugs eat fungi that live on dead logs.

A stag beetle grub grows inside a rotting log for several years.

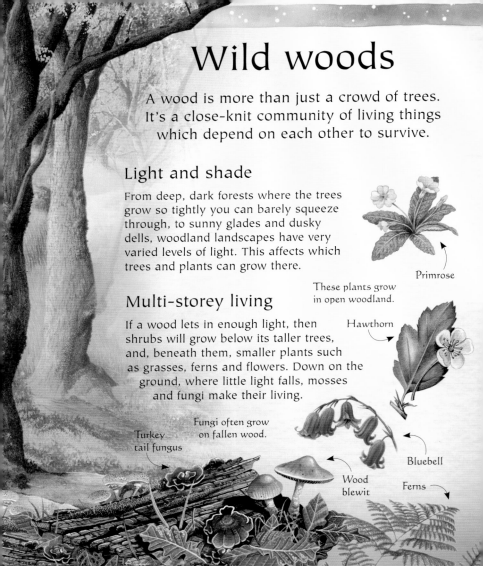

Wild woods

A wood is more than just a crowd of trees.
It's a close-knit community of living things
which depend on each other to survive.

Light and shade

From deep, dark forests where the trees
grow so tightly you can barely squeeze
through, to sunny glades and dusky
dells, woodland landscapes have very
varied levels of light. This affects which
trees and plants can grow there.

Primrose

These plants grow
in open woodland.

Multi-storey living

If a wood lets in enough light, then
shrubs will grow below its taller trees,
and, beneath them, smaller plants such
as grasses, ferns and flowers. Down on the
ground, where little light falls, mosses
and fungi make their living.

Hawthorn

Fungi often grow
on fallen wood.

Turkey
tail fungus

Bluebell

Wood
blewit

Ferns

Web of life

Just as a spider's web would fall apart if
its strands weren't all joined together, so
all the trees and animals in a wood need
each other to survive. If even one species
vanishes, many others can be affected.

1. In spring, fresh, young
leaves make a tasty
banquet for hungry
sawfly larvae.

3. Taking flight from their
treetop nests, sparrowhawks
weave through the trees as they
hunt great tits and other small birds.

2. Great tits live among the
shrubs. They may take 300 larvae
in a day, to feed their chicks.

Wriggling recyclers

In nature, nothing is wasted. Even
dead leaves are recycled. Earthworms
and other creepy-crawlies eat them
and help to break them down into
humus, a dark, rich soil ingredient
that helps the trees grow.

Shrews have to
eat every few
hours. This
one is sniffing
out juicy worms.

Worms tug dead
leaves down into
the soil, to plug
their burrows,
and to eat.

Bark life

Bark is always worth a second look. You might spot all sorts of tiny creatures crawling or scuttling up and down a trunk, or hiding in the nooks and crannies of its craggy surface.

Pine weevils eat the thin bark of young conifers.

This purple emperor butterfly is sucking sugary sap from broken bark with its straw-like mouthparts.

Litter bugs

The leaf litter covering a forest floor is teeming with life. Countless creatures rely on the fallen leaves for food and shelter. The leaf piles make ideal breeding and feeding grounds for moulds and other fungi, too.

Millipedes munch fallen leaves.

These white speckles are mould, which feeds on dead leaves, helping them to rot.

You might spot these creatures lurking in leaf litter.

Snail

Centipede

Most of this leaf has rotted away, leaving a delicate skeleton of lacy veins.

Woodland detective

Next time you go for a walk in the woods, keep your eyes open for clues that wildlife has been around.

This pine cone's seeds were roughly plucked out by a woodpecker.

The white squiggles on this bramble leaf are tunnels made by a tiny caterpillar called a leaf miner.

These hazelnuts have been nibbled by animals in their own special ways:

Dormouse

Grey squirrel

Wood mouse

Hazel

You may see bare branches where voles or squirrels have gnawed off the bark, as this bank vole is doing.

Dropping hints

Droppings are a sure sign that animals have passed by. Meat-eating animals leave sausage-shaped droppings with pointed ends. The droppings of plant-eaters are usually small and round.

Fallow deer droppings stick together in summer.

Rabbit droppings

Field vole droppings

Weasel droppings

Winter dropping

Hangers-on

Many living things survive by growing on others.
Most live harmlessly on their "hosts", but some, called
parasites, hurt them. A few actually give help in return.

Fungi

Mushrooms and toadstools belong to a
group of living things called fungi that,
unlike plants, can't make their own
food. Most of a fungus is unseen: a
tangled mass of root-like threads
that delve into wood or soil, slowly
digesting the matter around them.

A fly agaric's underground
threads fuse with
nearby birch tree
roots, passing vital
minerals to the tree
and taking extra food
from it in return.

Friend or foe?

Fungi such as fly agaric help
trees survive. Some bracket
fungi, on the other hand,
are parasites that may
eventually kill them.

Honey fungus like
this may grow on
dead or living trees,
steadily rotting
their wood.

Beef steak
bracket grows on
oak, doing little harm.

Birch bracket
gradually kills
the birch trees
on which it lives.

A leg up

Some plants use trees for physical support, twisting and climbing around them to reach the light. Ivy does no harm, but parasites such as mistletoe can weaken a tree.

Ivy is an evergreen plant that is often seen on trees, as well as walls and houses.

Mistletoe sucks watery sap from trees, like a vampire drinking blood.

Common polypody is a fern that sometimes grows on branches.

White berries

Leafy lichen

Crusty growths

While fungi can't make food, microscopic plants called algae can. Some fungi and algae team up to form crusty growths called lichens. These often grow on old trees with ridged bark, such as oak.

Lichen only grows where the air is clean. The more leafy or branching the type of lichen, the purer the air.

Branching lichen

Bog moss (close-up)

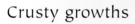

Cushion moss

Moist moss

Moss is a simple, flowerless plant that grows best in damp places. It is often found clinging to the shadiest side of old tree trunks.

Pine woods

Pines are conifers that can grow well in places with poor soil. There are some very old, natural pine woods, but most were planted by people.

Room to grow

Most planted pine forests are dark, crowded, and littered with tough pine needles, allowing few plants to grow. But in ancient Scots pine woods that have grown naturally, there are sunny clearings where a few hardy plants can survive.

Unlike most conifers, mature Scots pines aren't cone-shaped, but often have an uneven, or flat-topped look.

Scots pines have tall trunks with reddish bark near the top.

These plants grow in old Scots pine woods.

Lower down, the bark is greyish and flaky.

Rowan berries in late summer

Twinflower

Downy birch catkins in spring

Sickener fungus breaks down pine needles, returning their goodness to the soil.

Juniper berries in autumn

Pine wildlife

Although life is hard for plants and animals in pine woods, some thrive there, and a few can only live among ancient pines.

Pine martens are rare animals related to stoats. They hunt birds and voles.

Crossbills use their overlapping beaks to tweak the seeds out of pine cones.

Long-eared owl

Red deer

Wood ants gather large mounds of pine needles to protect their nests.

Capercaillies are turkey-sized birds found only in Scottish pine woods.

Fox and cubs

Sticky stuff

Conifers, especially pines, produce a sticky, smelly, bitter substance called resin. It deters animals from eating them, traps attacking insects, and seals wounds in the wood.

Oak woods

Oaks have spreading branches with clumps of leaves, letting in plenty of light. This allows many plants and even other trees to flourish beneath them.

Home to hundreds

Oak trees, especially English oaks, provide food and shelter to hundreds of different living things, from squirrels and birds, to butterflies, wasps, mosses and fungi. Ancient oak woods contain the greatest mix of plants and animals.

Great spotted woodpecker

Wood anemone

Bluebell

Badger

Wood sorrel

All these living things may dwell in an oak wood. See how many kinds you can spot here.

Yellow archangel

Bramble

Timberman beetle

Insect wars

For many insects, oak leaves combine a source of food and a place to lay eggs. The trees fight back, filling their leaves with a chemical that's hard to digest. Oaks can make up for lost leaves with a new set in late summer, called their Lammas growth.

Purple hairstreak butterfly caterpillars look like oak buds.

These disguised caterpillars can feed on oak trees without being spotted by hungry birds.

Gall wasp

Spangle galls

Kidney galls

Great oak beauty moth caterpillars look like oak twigs.

Cherry galls

Oak apple galls

To defend itself, an oak grows hard swellings, called galls, around insect eggs. These house the growing grubs, and provide food when they hatch.

Green tortrix moth caterpillars munch their way through hundreds of oak leaves in early spring.

Acorns for all

In autumn, oak twigs are laden with shiny acorns. As well as containing the seeds of new trees, their nutty goodness helps sustain many animals through the winter.

English oak acorns grow on long stalks.

Sessile oak acorns have no stalks, sitting directly on the twig.

A jay may bury as many as 5,000 acorns as a winter supply. Some will grow into new oak trees.

Beech woods

Beech branches form a thick, leafy canopy which stops most of the light from reaching the woodland floor. Few plants are able to grow beneath them.

Life in the shade

Only a handful of trees, such as holly and yew, can thrive alongside beeches. They are evergreen, so they can make food from sunlight all year, and they grow very slowly, so they don't need as much energy as other plants.

Holly can survive in beech's heavy shade.

Brief blooms

Of the flowers that do grow in beech woods, many only last for the short, sunny spell between winter and spring. Others have found ways to endure the gloom.

Cuckoo pint has large leaves to gather as much light as possible.

Solomon's seal grows as tall as it can.

Common dog violet's dark green leaves have extra chlorophyll to make the most of dim light.

The early spring sunlight magically transforms this beech wood floor into a sea of bluebells.

Leafy carpet

Dead beech leaves are tough and take a long time to rot, so beech woods are usually carpeted in leaf litter. This makes it hard for most flowers to grow, but creepy-crawlies flourish.

Snails hide among the damp leaves by day, and feed on them by night.

Wood crickets prowl around, hunting smaller insects in the litter.

Bird's nest orchids don't need sunlight to grow, but live on dead leaves.

Beechnuts

In autumn, beechnuts ripen. Their prickly cases start to split, and the nuts tumble to the woodland floor, where many are gratefully gobbled up by hungry wildlife.

Beechnuts are three-sided and are protected by bristly husks.

A nuthatch makes beechnuts "hatch" out by jamming them into bark and hammering them with its beak.

Wet woods

Most trees can't survive in waterlogged soil, but a few, such as willow and alder, thrive in marshy areas, or alongside rivers and streams.

Watery willows

Boggy woodland covered with willows and alders is known as carr. It is full of water-loving plants, and lush undergrowth where animals and birds can scurry in safety.

Goat willow

Alder

Great reedmace

Common reed

Brooklime

You can find these plants in wet woods.

Alders have small, cone-like fruits.

Common nettle

Meadowsweet

Sailing seeds

Alders, poplars and willows near water drop oily-coated seeds onto its surface. These float away, washing up on other banks, and may sprout into new trees.

Alder seeds

112

Ferns

Ferns have been around since prehistoric times. Their large, leafy fronds come in many shapes, from feathery bracken to glossy, crinkled hart's-tongue. Underneath the fronds, you may see tiny, brown clumps of seed-like spores.

Bracken

Ferns grow abundantly in damp places.

Every species has a different pattern of spores.

Spores on bracken

Hard fern

Hart's-tongue fern

Leaf beetle

Redpolls feed on seeds in spring.

Otters and others

Unsurprisingly, wet woods are home to many animals, from frisky otters that fish in the water, to birds such as redpolls, that feast on alder seeds. You'll also find countless insects.

An otter snoozes on a willow branch hanging over a lazy river.

Dragonflies rest on willow leaves in summer.

Cranefly

Town trees

Even if you live in a built-up area, you probably won't have to go far to see trees. They are planted in towns and cities to provide pleasant scenery, but do a whole lot more.

Trees of peace

Trees can help people to relax, and take pride in the places where they live and work. Research has shown that hospital patients recover more quickly when they can see trees, and police report fewer crimes in leafy areas.

Trees attract songbirds and help to muffle traffic noise.

Starling

Plant wisely

If trees are chosen carefully, they can bring many benefits to towns, but trees planted in the wrong places can cause problems.

Rowans have pretty, red berries in summer, but these can make pavements slippery.

In summer, common lime trees give shelter, but also drip with honeydew, a sticky goo made by the aphids that live on them.

London planes grow very well in cities, but their roots can cause pavements to buckle.

Beech offers deep shade, but blocks out light where it's too close to houses.

Air fresheners

As well as producing the oxygen gas that people and animals breathe, some trees actually soak up the poisonous gases that pollute the air of towns and cities.

The bark of London plane withstands air pollution, flaking off regularly to rid itself of harmful chemicals.

These trees help to clean up city pollution.

Field maple

Silver birch

Street survivors

City life can be hard on trees: their branches are often bashed by buses and their roots squashed beneath pavements. They also have to put up with car fumes, vandalism and frequent pruning. Some trees survive cities better than others.

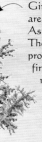

Ginkgoes are unique Asian trees. They are insect-proof and can resist fire, pollution and even nuclear disasters.

Flowering cherry trees like these, planted for their candy-pink blossom, are unlikely to live their full life spans in the parched, paved city streets.

Wood is good

Even in the 21st century, no one has invented a
better building material than wood. It is strong,
tough and light – and it's very easy to grow.

From log to plank

Trunks and big branches felled
for wood are called timber. The
logs are taken by truck or boat
to sawmills. Each one is sawn
in a way that makes as many
useful planks as possible.

These will be the
widest planks.

Heartwood is
strong, and used
as building timber.

Leftover wood chips
are pulped to make
paper. Bark chippings
are used in gardening
and as animal bedding.

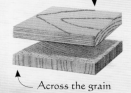

Along the grain

Across the grain

Grain

Every plank has a pattern of lines and whorls,
called its grain, made by the yearly growth
rings inside the tree. Wood is at its strongest
when it is cut along the grain. Cut across the
grain, it's more likely to crack and break.

Knots

Base of a branch

Some planks have
dark spots, called
knots, where the base
of a branch was buried
in the tree trunk. Knots
can weaken wood, but
they may also make it
look more attractive.

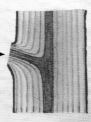

This trunk
has been cut
lengthways.

Uses of wood

Conifers grow quickly, and their wood, known as softwood, is plentiful. It is used where large quantities of timber are needed, such as for building and paper making. Broadleaved trees grow at a much gentler pace, producing tough, resilient "hardwood". This is often used in making furniture, flooring and musical instruments.

The colour, strength and suppleness of these trees makes their wood useful for different purposes.

This violin was crafted from a number of woods, each one selected for its qualities.

Cherry wood is used to make fine furniture.

Solid and sturdy, oak is ideal for beams and floors.

Spruce carries sound well and is used in instrument making.

Processed wood

A lot of the wood you see has been processed to strengthen it, or to produce items more quickly and cheaply than it's possible to do using natural wood.

Grain

Veneer

Cutting blade

Plywood is thin layers of wood glued together to make it stronger.

Veneer is a thin sheet of wood with a decorative grain, glued onto cheap, plain wood.

Forest harvest

People have always harvested trees for their wood, but they provide much more besides.

Fruit 'n' nut

It's not just animals that eat fruit and nuts. People relish their sweet flavours, and need the vital vitamins and nourishment they give.

Walnuts can help keep your heart healthy.

Walnuts grow in leathery, green jackets.

Sweet chestnuts are often roasted before eating.

These succulent plums are brimful of vitamins which can help your body fight disease.

Healing trees

Lots of trees contain chemicals that scientists have developed into medicines. Aspirin, used to soothe headaches and fevers, is based on a chemical found in willow bark.

Oil from eucalyptus leaves is used in cough and cold remedies.

A chemical in yew bark is used to fight cancer.

Cinnamon bark

Juniper berries

Bay leaves

Herbs and spices

Many parts of trees are used in cooking. The leaves of bay laurel add a savoury tang to soups and stews. The bark of cinnamon trees is ground into a fragrant spice, and juniper trees have berry-like fruits which are dried and used to season strongly flavoured meats.

Silkworms

The leaves of white mulberry trees provide a home and food for silk moth caterpillars. These spin cocoons with a soft, strong thread, which can be woven into the finest, shimmering silks.

White mulberry leaves

Silkworm

A single silkworm cocoon can contain up to 900m (3,000ft) of unbroken silk thread.

Silkworms turn into silk moths.

Snuffle a truffle

Although many woodland fungi are poisonous, a few are edible. Some, such as porcini and chanterelle, are fairly common. Truffles are rare, potato-shaped fungi that grow under tree roots. They are highly prized because they're difficult to find.

Chanterelle mushrooms often grow by beech trees.

Porcini mushrooms are also known as ceps or penny buns.

Black truffle

In Italy and France, pigs are trained to sniff out truffles.

Working with trees

People have worked with trees for centuries, planting and pruning them to grow in useful ways. Most woods have been carefully managed for at least part of their lifetime.

Traditional trimming

Coppicing is an ancient way of managing trees by cutting them down to a stump, or "stool". Multiple shoots then grow into straight sticks which have many uses, from basket-making to building.

The shoots of a coppiced stump grow long and straight.

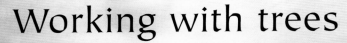

In another old method, pollarding, the tops of trees are cut off some way above the ground so grazing animals can't eat their shoots. Trees in towns are often pollarded so they don't overshadow houses, or tangle in overhead wires.

A farmer has pollarded this row of willow trees to produce a harvest of useful sticks, called wands or withies.

Forestry today

Forestry is about farming trees for timber, both in wild woods and in man-made ones, called plantations. Foresters use various methods to ensure new crops of trees will grow.

Mechanical tree harvesters, like this, have a rotating arm to grip large trunks, and a circular saw to cut them up.

In clearcutting, a small patch of trees is felled. Those left produce seeds for new trees.

The seed tree system takes trees from a wide area, leaving a few behind for reseeding.

In selective felling, the strongest trees are left to grow longest, to produce wood of the best quality.

Planting out

To prepare a new plantation, ground must first be cleared and ploughed. Young trees are planted about 4m apart: that's about 63,000 trees in a square kilometre.

Seedlings are planted out when they are about 20 times as tall as this picture.

Changing times

Plantations of conifers grow more quickly than broadleaf ones, making for more regular harvests, but few animals can live in them. Conifer plantations were once most common but today, foresters plant more broadleaves, and care for wildlife.

Plantation of conifers

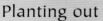

Protecting trees

Sustainable forestry is a way of working that carefully controls the pace at which trees are felled and replanted, to keep forests and their wildlife healthy for the future.

Vanishing forests

Forests, especially tropical rainforests, are not always looked after in a sustainable way. Around the world, every minute, an area of trees the size of 37 football pitches is lost as forests are cleared for farmland, or harvested to make timber or fuel.

In some places, only certain trees are selected for logging. This allows the forest to regrow at its own pace.

"Slash and burn" is a way of creating farmland by felling and burning trees. Crops grow for a short time, but soon the dusty soil is useless, so more land is needed and more trees must be sacrificed.

Chopping down trees is an easy way to make money, even where it is illegal.

No place like home

Tropical rainforests are huge, evergreen, broadleaf forests in hot, wet parts of South America, Africa and Asia. They are home to the world's greatest variety of life, but are being wiped out faster than any other forests. Amazing animals and valuable plants are in danger of dying out.

The forest home of these orang-utans in Borneo is being destroyed so quickly, to make oil palm plantations, that they may die out in the next five years.

Poison arrow frogs are made homeless as the rainforest vanishes.

Rosy periwinkles are rare rainforest flowers, used to make cancer medicine.

What can you do?

You can help save the world's trees by being careful how you use tree products:

- Use both sides of a piece of paper.
- Use recycled paper: it's made from used paper so it doesn't harm any more trees.
- Recycle as much paper as you can yourself.
- Check that paper and wood products you use are labelled "sustainable", or have a mark proving they came from well-managed forests.

This mark shows paper is made from wood from well-managed forests.

This symbol means that a product can be recycled.

Trees of the world

Around the globe, trees grow in surprising ways as they adapt to life in extremely varied conditions.

North America

The USA is home to some very tough trees. Joshua trees are spiky-leaved evergreens that survive in the parched Mojave desert. In Florida, mangrove trees and swamp cypresses flourish in the salty, coastal swamps. In California, ancient giant sequoias tower over all other plant life.

Mangroves prop themselves up above the water on stilt-like roots, as you can see here.

The branches of a Joshua tree bend in a new direction whenever a clump of fresh blossoms grows.

Green needles

Swamp cypress needles are usually green but, in autumn, they turn a fiery red before dropping off the tree.

Europe

Tamarisks grow by windy seashores in many parts of Europe, and maritime pines thrive in Mediterranean areas. In the Canary Islands, near Morocco, umbrella-shaped dragon trees are found.

Dragon trees take their name from their sticky red resin, known as dragon's blood, which is used as a dye.

In summer, tamarisks are covered in clusters of tiny pink flowers.

Tamarisk

Maritime pines are planted on sand dunes, to help stop the sand blowing away.

Australasia

In the dry, outback regions of Australia, eucalyptus trees thrive. They grow long roots to suck up water deep under the ground. The roots also store water for the tree to use in times of drought. A type of eucalyptus called a mountain ash can be found in cooler, mountainous areas of southern Australasia.

Australian mountain ashes are the tallest hardwood trees in the world.

Eucalyptus leaves have a tough covering that prevents them from losing too much water.

South America

The rainforests of Brazil contain a vast array of plant life, including towering giants, such as red meranti, and cacao trees, from which chocolate is made. Many types of rainforest tree are of great use to people, providing food, medicine and materials.

Banana flowers hang down from long stalks.

Unripe banana fruit

Banana flower

Mango

Many kinds of exotic fruits grow in rainforests.

Papaya

Guava

Passion fruit

Cacao tree flowers grow on the trunk, and turn into pod-like fruit.

Rainforest trees grow to varying heights, forming different layers.

The pods hold seeds that are used to make chocolate.

Some very tall rainforest trees only have shallow roots. Their trunks flare out at the base for extra support.

Asia

In the Middle East, date palms have been grown for over 8000 years, and the trees are said to have 800 different uses. Asian banyans, or "strangler figs", start life on the branches of another tree. Their roots snake groundwards around the trunk, until they eventually smother their host to death, and the banyan takes its place.

Banyans are some of the world's widest trees.

Date palms need a hot climate to bear fruit, but also tend to grow near a source of water.

Africa

African acacias have a parasol shape because all their lower leaves are eaten by giraffes. Baobabs, nicknamed "upside-down trees", are tubby trees whose spindly twigs look like roots waving in the air.

Baobabs can store enough water in their thick trunks to last for nine months without rain.

On many African plains, acacias are all that grow.

Myths and legends

There's something mysterious about trees. They've inspired countless myths and magical stories, and are important symbols in many religions.

Robin Hood

The legends of the cunning outlaw Robin Hood centre on Sherwood Forest in England. He and his companions, the Merry Men, are said to have hidden in its green depths from the wicked Sheriff of Nottingham. A tree called the Major Oak, alive today, is said to have been their hideout.

Robin Hood is said to have dressed in green to hide among the trees of Sherwood Forest.

Tears and flowers

In one Greek myth, a princess, Phyllis, loved a soldier named Acamas. He went off to war for ten years, and she nearly died of heartbreak. A kind goddess saved Phyllis by turning her into an almond tree. On his return, Acamas sadly kissed the leafless tree. All at once, it burst into flower.

Almond trees blossom before their leaves appear. The story of Phyllis tells why.

A German legend

One Christmas night, Martin Luther, a churchman, was walking home through the woods. Inspired by the starlight twinkling in the trees, he took a little fir tree home to his family, and set candles in its branches to represent the stars.

The two trees

The Bible tells the story of the Garden of Eden. God told Adam and Eve, the first people, that they might eat the fruit of any tree except the Tree of the Knowledge of Good and Evil. They disobeyed God, and were banished from Eden, so they could not eat from the Tree of Life, which would have let them live forever.

A sly serpent misled Eve by twisting God's words, and she ate the fruit of the forbidden tree.

The world tree

The Vikings believed that the universe was held together by the roots of a giant ash tree, named Yggdrasil. One root passed through Asgard, the dwelling-place of gods and elves. Another ran through Midgard, the human world, and the last plunged into Niflheim, the frozen land of the dead.

Yggdrasil, the cosmic ash

Amazing but true

Time traveller

Ginkgoes are Chinese trees that lived before the dinosaurs. Fossils show that prehistoric ginkgoes were very similar to those alive today.

Ginkgo

Fossilized leaf of an early ginkgo

Mexican marvel

In Oaxaca, Mexico, is the world's fattest tree. Known as the Tule Tree, this Montezuma cypress is 35.8m (117½ ft) around. It takes 26 men holding hands to encircle its trunk.

Medicine trees

A quarter of all medicines contain chemicals found in trees and plants from the steamy rainforests of South America and Asia.

Many rainforest plants have healing power.

Reach for the sky

The world's tallest tree is a coast redwood in California, USA. Named Hyperion, it is 115.2m (378ft) high – taller than London's Big Ben.

Coast redwood

General giant

General Sherman, a giant sequoia, is the bulkiest living thing on Earth. Growing in Sequoia National Park, California, it measures 83.8m (275ft) high by 31.3m (102½ ft) around the base.

Supersize cone

The longest cones come from sugar pines, which grow in the USA. They can measure 66cm (26in) – that's over two-thirds the length of a cricket bat.

Sugar pine cone

Mammoth fruit

The jackfruit tree of India has the largest fruit of any broadleaf or conifer. The prickly, yellow-green fruit can be up to 90cm (35in) long and 50cm (20in) wide, and weigh 34kg (75lb) – as much as a ten-year-old boy.

These ripening jackfruit smell like rotting onions, but taste more like pineapple.

Protection points

African acacias guard their leaves with thorns, but giraffes still reach them with their long, flexible tongues. So, as soon as the nibbling begins, the trees produce a foul-tasting chemical. The giraffes soon leave to find a tastier tree.

Thorns

Bristlecone pine

Old as the hills

Bristlecone pines in the dry, harsh surroundings of the Californian White Mountains can only survive by growing very slowly. One pine, nicknamed Methuselah, is over 4,770 years old. It was a seedling when the pyramids of Egypt were being built.

Digging deep

One wild fig tree in South Africa was found to have roots tunnelling down to 120m (400ft) underground.

Far-flung forest

Earth's largest stretch of unbroken forest is the East Siberian taiga. With an area of 3,900,000km^2 (1,500,000 square miles), it covers over a fifth of Russia.

Ant apartment

A bullhorn acacia has a special relationship with ants. It lets an army of the insects live inside its huge thorns, and even makes tiny food parcels for them. In return, the ants sting animals that try to eat the tree.

This ant has collected a food parcel from its host's leaf-tips.

Food parcels

Shoots from roots

English elm fruits hold seeds, but they are infertile, which means new trees won't grow from them. Instead, elms spread by sending up new shoots from their roots.

Elm seed

Moon trees

In 1971, astronauts took seeds from different types of trees to the Moon to see how they would be affected. When they returned to Earth, scientists planted the seeds and nearly all grew successfully. The resulting trees were nicknamed "Moon trees".

Sycamore and Douglas fir seeds have been to the Moon and back.

Douglas fir seeds

Sycamore seeds

Dinosaur defence

Chilean pines, also known as monkey puzzle trees, have been around for many millions of years. Some experts think that their tangled branches and dagger-like leaves evolved to stop hungry dinosaurs munching on them.

This modern Chilean pine looks similar to its prehistoric ancestors.

Tree fuel

Copaiba tree sap is almost the same as diesel fuel and can be poured straight into a truck's tank. In one day, 100 millitres (1/5 pint) can be collected from a single tree.

Long flight

Cottonwood seeds can float in the air for days. Each tiny seed is surrounded by white, fluffy hairs that help it to catch even the gentlest of breezes.

Chemical warfare

If a willow is being eaten by an animal, it releases a chemical into the air. This alerts the willows nearby, which then pump their leaves full of chemicals that make the leaves indigestible to animals.

Crack willow leaves

Fireproof

Trees with thick bark, such as pine and sequoia, can survive fierce forest fires. These tough trees are only scarred by the flames and their wood is unharmed.

Sailing seeds

In salty swamps, seeds from mangrove trees drop into the water. Some can float for up to a year before finding a good spot to grow. Other types of mangrove seeds begin to grow while still attached to their parents, then float away when they are seedlings.

Shortest trees

In the frozen Arctic tundra, trees are so blasted by the wind that their branches cling to the ground. Ground willow can grow 5m (16½ft) long, but only grows 10cm (4in) high.

Ground willow branches twist and turn close to the ground.

Disappearing forests

10,000 years ago, around half of the Earth's land surface was covered by forest. Today, forests cover only 30% of the land.

After dropping from the tree, mangrove seeds float away, aided by the wind and water currents.

Flowers

A history of flowers

Flowers have played an important role in people's lives for thousands of years. They have formed part of festivals and rituals, inspired artists, poets and storytellers and even been used as charms for love and luck.

Flowers for all occasions

For many people, the most important feature of a flower is its beauty. This is why flowers are so popular as decorations or ornaments, and are given as gifts to cheer people up. But flowers have other more practical uses, too, as ingredients in perfumes, foods and medicines. You can find out more about these on pages 186–189.

Roses have been specially grown for their looks for over 5,000 years.

Flower symbols

Flowers have been used to symbolize feelings and ideas for many centuries. In the past, when most people couldn't read or write, flower symbolism was a language that everyone understood.

Lilies were used in religious paintings to stand for purity.

Flower emblems

Many countries, states and regions have their own floral emblems. Some are common flowers in that area, but others are connected with a historical person or event.

These are cornflowers. Emperor Wilhelm of Germany liked them so much, he made them the national flower.

Floral design

The pleasing shapes of flowers have always inspired artists and craftworkers. In 19th-century Britain, artist William Morris became well-known for basing his designs on flowers and plants.

A wallpaper pattern inspired by William Morris's curling flower and leaf shapes

Flowers and rituals

Using flowers in religious ceremonies and other rituals is a tradition followed throughout history. Flower remains have been found in 60,000-year-old graves, and flowers are still given or carried at weddings or funerals in most parts of the world today.

The flowers in a wedding bouquet symbolize the bride's love and faithfulness to her partner.

Looking at flowers

Plants grow flowers as part of the process of making more plants like themselves. Flowers come in hundreds of shapes and sizes, and are found in most of the world's landscapes.

What do flowers do?

Flowers make tiny grains called pollen, which is carried to other flowers by insects and animals, or by the wind. The flower that receives it can then develop seeds, which will grow into new plants. Some flowers reward their visitors with a sweet liquid called nectar.

This anemone's bright petals attract insects.

Flower parts

Pollen is made by a flower's male parts, called stamens. Its female part, called the pistil, contains the structures that will later become seeds. Some flowers have only male or only female parts, but most have both.

You can see the pistil and stamens in the middle of the anemone.

Male and female parts vary in appearance from plant to plant. This is what an anemone's pistil and stamens look like close-up.

Bottlebrush flowers have hundreds of stamens.

A horned poppy has a long, slim pistil and small stamens.

Stamens

Pistil

*

These white blossoms will one day produce apples.

Tree flowers

Most people think of flowers as growing on small plants, but trees produce them too. In spring, many grow delicate blossoms, which later turn into fruits, nuts or berries. These hold seeds inside, protected by juicy layers or a hard shell.

Survival skills

Most experts think that flowering plants first grew over 130 million years ago. Today, there are around 270,000 types around the world. They have survived so well, and spread so far, because of their ability to thrive in the unlikeliest of places.

*

European edelweiss lives on cold, dry mountains. It has a thick layer of hairs to trap heat and water.

Water hyacinths have swollen, air-filled leaves, allowing them to float on water.

*

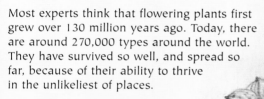

This rainforest orchid gets the light it needs by attaching itself to a branch near the top of a tree.

Flower features

If you want to identify a plant that you've found, look at where it grows, the number of flowers it has, and the shape and arrangement of its petals and leaves. You can then look it up in a field guide, or on the internet.

Height and width

Flowers can grow up into the air, or creep sideways and cover the ground. A plant that spreads out like this is called a mat-forming plant.

Many garden flowers, like these lupins, grow upright.

This creeping jenny is a mat-forming plant.

Flowers and stems

Plants might have one flower on a single stem, or many small flowers growing in a bunch.

Primroses have one flower per stem.

Rock cress has flowers in bunches.

Flowers within flowers

Sometimes, what you might think is a single flower is actually made up of lots of smaller flowers, called florets.

Asters are made up of many florets.

The florets in the middle are tiny yellow flowers.

Each floret around the outside has one long petal.

Location

Most flowers need certain conditions in order to grow well. For instance, they might prefer a shady rather than a sunny place, or damp soil rather than dry.

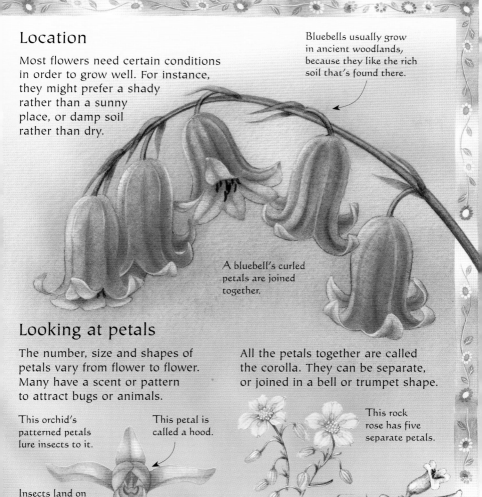

Bluebells usually grow in ancient woodlands, because they like the rich soil that's found there.

A bluebell's curled petals are joined together.

Looking at petals

The number, size and shapes of petals vary from flower to flower. Many have a scent or pattern to attract bugs or animals.

All the petals together are called the corolla. They can be separate, or joined in a bell or trumpet shape.

This orchid's patterned petals lure insects to it.

This petal is called a hood.

This rock rose has five separate petals.

Insects land on this petal, the lip.

*

Beardtongue flowers have joined petals.

Leaves

If you find a plant whose flowers have not yet opened, you might still be able to identify it by the look of its leaves. See if they have one overall shape, or are made up of several parts. Sometimes, there are many tiny leaves on one stalk.

Each of these bugle leaves is one large shape.

A wood anemone's leaf divides into three parts, joined at the base.

Partridge-pea flowers have little leaves, called leaflets, on a single stalk.

Shapes and edges

Leaves come in many different shapes, and their outlines can be smooth, wavy, sharp or jagged.

Pheasant's eye flowers have feathery leaves.

Lesser celandine has smooth, heart-shaped leaves.

Toothed leaves, like a wild strawberry's, are jagged.

A flowering currant's leaves are lobed, which means they are partially divided.

Winter squill leaves are entire (not toothed or lobed).

Sea holly's leaves are spiky.

Leaf arrangements

Look out for the different ways in which leaves can be arranged on the stem of a plant.

The leaves of a pussy paw form a rosette at the base of its stem.

Rose-pink leaves grow in opposite pairs.

Scarlet paintbrush leaves grow alternately on each side of the stem.

The leaves of an ice plant grow up the stem in a pattern like a spiral staircase.

Wood lily leaves grow in rings called whorls.

Leaf rubbing

Leaves from garden flowers can be used to make decorative leaf rubbings.

You will need:

❀ plain paper ❀ pencils or crayons ❀ clean, dry leaves

1. Place one or more leaves on a sheet of paper.

2. Carefully place more paper on top. Rub gently on it with a crayon.

You could arrange several leaves in a pattern before rubbing them.

How flowers grow

Most flowering plants start life as seeds. These sprout into shoots, and eventually grow flowers, which in turn make more seeds so the whole cycle can start again. This page shows how a poppy grows.

Most types of flowers develop in the same way as poppies.

Bud

1. In the spring, a poppy plant grows from a seed. First, it grows leaves. Then, buds start to form, with flowers furled up inside them.

2. Each flower is protected by tough sepals. These begin to part as the flower grows.

Each poppy bud has two spiky sepals.

Common poppy

3. In the summer, the flower's petals open out. You can see its male and female parts – the stamens and pistil – in the middle.

The pistil has two parts: a sticky stigma on top, and an ovary beneath.

Stamens

Pistil

*

Stigma

Ovary

Stamens have pod-like anthers on the end of long, spindly filaments. The anthers open to release grains of pollen.

Anther

Pollen grains

Filament

4. Bees and other pollen-carriers are attracted to poppies by their bright red petals. Pollen from the anthers sticks to the bee's hairy body as it crawls over the flower.

5. If the bee visits another poppy, the pollen may rub off its body onto the other flower's stigma. The next page shows what happens after this stage, which is called pollination, has taken place.

6. When grains of poppy pollen land on another poppy's stigma, very thin tubes begin to grow out of them, down to the ovary.

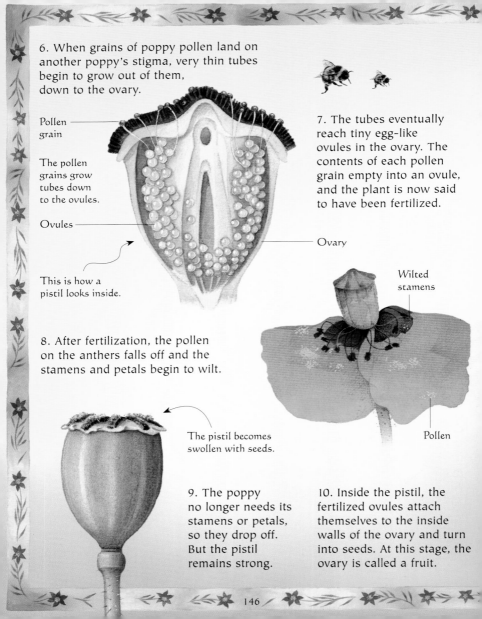

Pollen grain

The pollen grains grow tubes down to the ovules.

Ovules

This is how a pistil looks inside.

7. The tubes eventually reach tiny egg-like ovules in the ovary. The contents of each pollen grain empty into an ovule, and the plant is now said to have been fertilized.

Ovary

Wilted stamens

8. After fertilization, the pollen on the anthers falls off and the stamens and petals begin to wilt.

Pollen

The pistil becomes swollen with seeds.

9. The poppy no longer needs its stamens or petals, so they drop off. But the pistil remains strong.

10. Inside the pistil, the fertilized ovules attach themselves to the inside walls of the ovary and turn into seeds. At this stage, the ovary is called a fruit.

11. As the poppy fruit ripens, its outer case dries up. Holes appear at the top to let the seeds out.

Hole

Seeds

12. The seeds break away from the walls inside the fruit. When the poppy is blown about by the wind, the seeds are scattered like pepper from a pepper shaker.

13. Any seeds that fall out of the fruit onto the soil can grow into new plants next spring. These in turn will make seeds of their own.

Pollen from a poppy can't make seeds in buttercups, or any flower other than another poppy.

Spreading pollen

Most flowers can't pollinate themselves, because their stigmas and stamens ripen at different times. Instead, their pollen is carried off by animals, or by the wind.

Animal attraction

The strong, sweet smell of this stargazer lily lets passing insects know that it's worth paying a visit.

Patterns on the flower's petals, called nectar guides, show insects where to find the nectar.

These spots and stripes are nectar guides.

Some types of flowers have nectar guides that only bees can see.

This evening primrose flower looks plain to you...

...but a bee's ultraviolet vision sees the nectar guides clearly.

A bird of paradise flower attracts birds. Its pollen sticks to their feet as they land.

Blowing in the wind

Flowers that rely on the wind to carry their pollen usually have uncovered stamens and pistils. Most of them hang loosely down, so it's easier for the wind to blow them about.

Each of these catkins is made up of dozens of tiny flowers. They give out lots of pollen, to increase the chances of it being blown to the right place.

Self-pollination

A few kinds of flowers use insects, but can also pollinate themselves.

Male Eucera bee

Pollen sacs

Stamens

The stigma is hidden inside.

1. Bee orchids look and smell like female Eucera bees. Male bees are attracted to them.

2. When a male bee visits an orchid, pollen sacs stick to his head. He will carry this pollen to another orchid.

3. If no bees come, the orchid pollinates itself. Its stamens bend over, so the pollen sacs can touch the stigma.

Pollen protection

Flowers can't reproduce without their pollen, so they use clever tricks to keep it safe and dry, and make sure that only the right kind of animals take it away.

Garden guardians

Some flowers only open when the weather is warm and sunny. They close up again if it looks like rain.

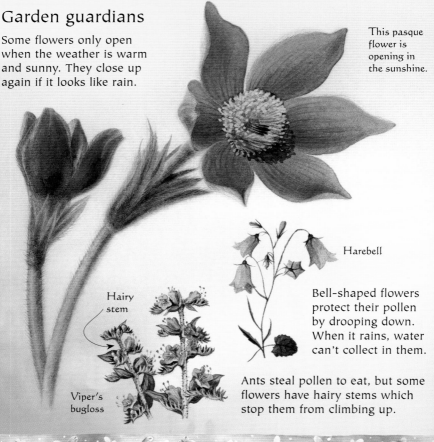

This pasque flower is opening in the sunshine.

Harebell

Bell-shaped flowers protect their pollen by drooping down. When it rains, water can't collect in them.

Hairy stem

Viper's bugloss

Ants steal pollen to eat, but some flowers have hairy stems which stop them from climbing up.

Invitation only

Some flowers only allow certain kinds of visitors, or can only be pollinated at a particular time.

Stamens

Penstemon flowers

Trumpet-shaped flowers are pollinated by hummingbirds and other creatures with long tongues. Pollen rubs off on their bodies as they reach in to drink the nectar.

Pollen rubs off on the hummingbird's head as it feeds.

Hummingbird hawk moth

Long-nosed bat

Honeysuckle

Most types of agave plant are pollinated only by bats with long, bristly tongues for lapping up nectar.

Agave flower

Honeysuckle flowers open in the evening, when the moths that pollinate them are awake. Their strong scent makes them easy to find in the dark.

Broom flower

Broom flowers stay tightly shut when small insects land on them. But if a heavy bumblebee stops by, its weight is enough to make the flower open up.

Scattering seeds

Seeds need light to grow, so they must be carried away from the shadow of their parent plant to survive. You might see seeds flying through the air, hitch-hiking on animals and people, or floating down a stream.

Flying away

Some seeds have natural parachute, balloon or wing-like shapes. These float in the wind.

Dandelion seeds are inside tiny fruits attached to fluffy parachutes.

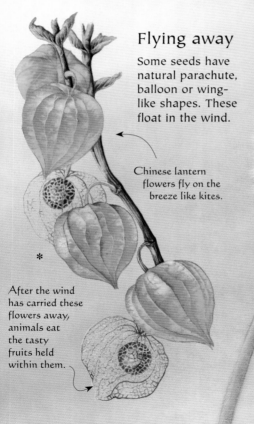

Chinese lantern flowers fly on the breeze like kites.

*

After the wind has carried these flowers away, animals eat the tasty fruits held within them.

Burdock seeds

Sticking on

Some seeds have burrs or hooks. They stick to animals, which carry them far away.

Tasty seeds

Birds and other animals eat fruits with seeds inside. Later, the seeds fall to the ground in their droppings.

This raccoon will spread the tree's seeds by eating its fruit.

Popping out

Some types of fruits burst open to shoot seeds out.

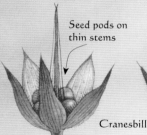

Seed pods on thin stems

Cranesbill

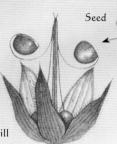

Seed

The stems curl up and shoot the seeds out of their pods.

On the water

A few types of seeds are carried away by oceans and rivers, inside floating pods.

People and seeds

People help to spread seeds too, often without even knowing. Seeds stick in the soles of shoes, or on car wheels.

Alder tree

Seeds fall in the water and float away.

In the garden

People have kept gardens for thousands of years. In the past, they were used to grow plants for food or medicine. Today, though, gardens are more likely to be full of flowers, which are grown for their appearance and scent.

Ornamental flowers

Many people like to grow ornamental flowers. These have been carefully bred to improve their shape and size, and they usually bloom for longer than their wild relatives.

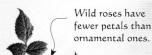

Wild roses have fewer petals than ornamental ones.

This tea rose was cultivated for its many delicate layers of pink petals.

Wild flowers

If something grows without being planted, it's probably a wild flower. Some types are harmless, but others spread very fast, stealing water and light from other plants. They are known as weeds.

Bindweed looks pretty, but its creeping stems choke other plants.

Types of flowers

When you're choosing what to plant in your garden, it helps to know what will bloom when. The three main kinds of flowering plants are annuals, biennials and perennials.

*

Plants that live and die in a single year are called annuals. Some grow, spread pollen and make seeds in as little as a week.

The seeds of annual plants, such as this petunia, stay buried in the ground over winter, and grow in the spring.

Biennials develop over two years. They grow in the first year, then make flowers and seeds in the second.

This wallflower is in its second year. The whole plant dies after it has made its seeds.

Plants that live for many years are called perennials.

Bellflowers are perennials. They regrow from roots each year.

Trees and shrubs, such as this buddleia, are perennials whose trunks and stems don't die each year.

Some perennials live underground as roots during winter, and grow new stems in the spring. Others keep their stems and trunks as well as their roots.

Growing sunflowers

Sunflowers attract bees and butterflies to your garden, and provide birds with tasty seeds to eat. If you plant seeds in early spring, you should have flowers by September.

You will need:

❀ small and large pots with holes in the bottom
❀ packet of sunflower seeds ❀ watering can
❀ potting compost ❀ small stones
❀ garden cane ❀ string or twine

Watering can

1. Put a handful of stones in the bottom of a small pot, and fill it with potting compost.

2. Press three or four sunflower seeds firmly into the compost.

3. Water the pot and put it outside in a light spot. Water it regularly so the compost doesn't dry out.

Small seedling

Large seedlings

4. A seedling should grow from each of the seeds. Take out all but the biggest two, so they have room to grow.

5. When the seedlings have grown about as tall as your hand, replant them into bigger pots.

6. Water your plants and leave them in a sunny place, out of the wind.

Twine

Cane

7. When the plants are about knee-high, push a cane into the compost in each pot. Tie the stems loosely on.

Some sunflowers can grow taller than a person. Check the seed packet to see what height yours might reach.

8. As the sunflowers grow taller, carefully tie their stems higher up the canes.

9. When the petals have fallen off, birds will eat the seeds in the middle.

Winter pansies

Pansies grow in cold weather, so you can use them to add a splash of brightness to a winter garden. They come in many shades, including purple, burgundy and gold.

When to plant

If you'd like to see winter flowers, sow your seeds in late summer. Some types of pansies should be sown in spring, so check the seed packet.

You will need:

✿ cardboard egg carton
✿ potting compost ✿ pansy seeds
✿ teaspoon ✿ strainer
✿ newspaper ✿ some pots

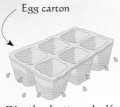

Egg carton

Strainer

1. Dip the bottom half of the carton in a bowl of water and let it drip.

2. Spoon compost into each section, but not all the way to the top.

3. Put two pansy seeds in each section. Sprinkle more compost on top.

Water the seeds regularly.

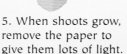

Shoots

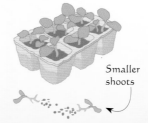

Smaller shoots

4. Cover the seeds with a newspaper. Keep them indoors in a cool spot.

5. When shoots grow, remove the paper to give them lots of light.

6. When each shoot has two leaves, pull out the smaller of the two shoots.

Roots

7. As your pansies grow, roots will sprout through the sides of the carton.

Handle the carton carefully as you pull.

8. Soak the carton in shallow water and gently pull the sections apart.

9. Put each section into a pot half-filled with compost. Fill in with more compost.

When flowers have started to grow, move your pots outside.

159

Flowers from leaves

In the right conditions, some plants can grow from a single leaf. Snipping a piece off a healthy plant and using it to create a new one is called taking a cutting, and it's a fun way to share plants with your friends.

You will need:

✿ African violet plant ✿ paper square ✿ scissors
✿ small bottle ✿ rubber band ✿ sharp pencil
✿ pot with holes in the bottom ✿ potting compost

1. Fill a small bottle with water. Don't fill it quite to the top.

2. Fasten the paper square over the top with a rubber band.

Choose a healthy-looking leaf from near the outside of the plant.

Scissors

Cut leaf

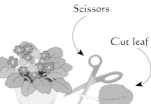

3. Use scissors to cut off a leaf, complete with its stalk, from an African violet plant.

Pencil

5. Hold the bottle and use the pencil to poke a hole in the middle of the paper.

6. Push the stalk through the hole until its end is in the water.

Keep your plant in a place with lots of light.

Roots

7. When tiny roots grow and new leaves appear, your leaf is ready to plant in a pot.

8. Fill the pot with compost, make a hole and put the plant in. Press the compost firmly all around.

9. Place the pot on a saucer. Water the plant by pouring water into the saucer.

Spring bulbs

Some plants grow from bulbs instead of seeds. A bulb has layers of tightly packed leaves inside, which store food for the plant. For spring flowers, plant bulbs in the autumn.

You will need:

✿ bulbs, such as crocus or daffodil
✿ frost-proof terracotta pot, three-quarters full of potting compost
✿ small stick ✿ trowel

Miniature daffodil

Crocus

1. Using the stick, make a hole in the compost for each bulb.

2. Rest the fat end of the bulbs in the holes.

3. Cover the bulbs with compost and put the pot outside.

Shoots appear first, then flowers will begin to grow after about 10–12 weeks.

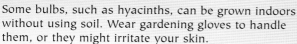

Some bulbs, such as hyacinths, can be grown indoors without using soil. Wear gardening gloves to handle them, or they might irritate your skin.

You will need:

✿ gardening gloves
✿ a hyacinth bulb
✿ three toothpicks
✿ a glass jar

When your bulb flowers, you can plant it in a pot. Keep it indoors.

Toothpick

1. Push toothpicks into the bulb. Fill the jar almost to the top with water.

2. Rest the toothpicks on the rim, so the bulb's fat end is near the water.

Roots

3. Leave the jar in a cool, dark place out of the frost, such as a shed.

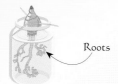

4. After roots have grown, leaves will sprout. Move the jar to a light, cool spot.

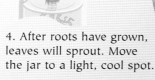

A miniature garden

If you'd like to see flowers without waiting for them to grow, you could buy ready-grown plants and make a mini garden.

You will need:

❀ plastic tray or bowl ❀ bag of small pebbles ❀ stones
❀ potting compost ❀ trowel ❀ gravel ❀ small plants and flowers
such as pansies, primulas, ivy, trailing lobelia and fittonia

1. Using the trowel, cover the bottom of the tray with about 2cm (1in) of pebbles.

2. Cover the layer of pebbles with potting compost. Fill the tray almost to the top.

3. Decide how you're going to lay out your plants. Leave a gap down the middle for a path.

4. Make holes in the compost for each plant. Take them from their pots and place them in.

5. Firmly press a little compost around each plant. Water them to help them settle.

6. Use the gravel to make a winding path through your garden. Add larger stones for decoration.

Garden care

Keep your garden indoors out of direct sunlight. Water it every other day, adding a little plant food to the water occasionally to help keep your plants healthy. If any plants grow too big for the tray, replant them into a larger pot.

A garden pond

If you like, you could add a pond to your garden by making a hole in the compost and putting in a plastic carton of water.

Put a little gravel in the carton, and fill it with water to make a pond.

Kalanchoe

Parlour palms

Primula flowers come in many shades.

Fittonia

Primulas

Trailing plants, such as ivy, hang over the sides.

This garden is decorated with stones, but you could also use toys, shells, or shiny glass pebbles.

Flower art

Flower shapes can be used to make pictures, or decorate cards, folders and diaries. Here are two easy types to create.

To make two-tone flowers, you will need:

❀ thick white paper ❀ water-based paints
❀ paintbrush with soft bristles
❀ jar of water

Use slightly watery paint.

Add the second shade quickly, while the petals are still wet.

The leaves should be near the petals, but not touching them.

1. Paint five blobs for petals, leaving a thin gap between them.

2. Add a contrasting shade of paint on each petal near the middle.

3. When the petals are dry, add leaves, and a blob in the middle.

Experiment with different paint shades.

Leave a thin white border around the flowers as you cut.

4. When all the paint has dried, cut the flowers and leaves out.

To make paper pansies, you will need:

❀ pink, purple, yellow, green and black tissue paper ❀ white paper or
thin cardboard ❀ glue ❀ scissors ❀ clean jar ❀ paintbrush

Make the
purple and
pink pieces
the size of a
large coin.

Leave a little
white area
around the
yellow paper.

1. Tear round shapes out
of the pink, purple, black
and yellow tissue paper.

2. Put a little glue
in the jar. Add a few
drops of water and stir.

3. Glue a small yellow
piece to the paper. Glue
two pink pieces above it.

Pansy leaves are
heart shaped,
like this.

4. Glue one purple
piece on either side of
the yellow paper, then
a bigger one beneath.

5. Glue black pieces onto
the petals. Cut out leaf
shapes and stick them
around the flowers.

Other pansy petal
combinations
that work well are
yellow and
blue, and red
and orange.

Pop-up flowers

Give your friends a surprise with this
pop-up flower display in a greeting card.

You will need:

❀ pieces of bright, stiff paper 18x28cm (7x11in), 8x10cm (3x4in) and
6x6cm (2.5x2.5in) ❀ extra sheet of paper ❀ painted flowers or flowers
cut from magazines and giftwrap ❀ glue ❀ scissors ❀ ruler

The largest piece (A)
will be your card.

1. Fold the largest (A)
and medium-sized (B)
pieces of paper in the
middle. Open them out.

Make each of these flaps
1cm (0.5in) wide.

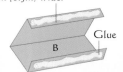

2. Make folds on the
ends of the medium
paper (B). Add glue to
the flaps' outer sides.

Match up the creases.

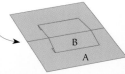

3. Turn piece B over
with the flaps tucked
under and press it flat
on the card's middle.

Match the crease on piece
C with the top of piece B.

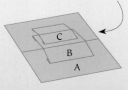

4. Repeat step 2 with
the smallest paper (C).
Glue it on top of piece
B and leave it to dry.

Find out how to paint flowers
like these on page 166.

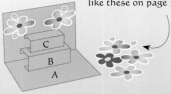

5. Glue a selection of
cut-out flowers and
leaves onto the card
above piece C.

Don't let any flowers overlap this edge.

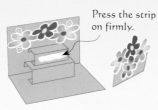

Press the strip on firmly.

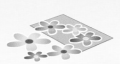

6. Cut out a piece of paper 5x9cm (2x3.5in). Glue flowers all over, except one long edge.

7. Glue the front of piece C. Press the paper strip onto it, with the straight edge at the bottom.

8. Cut out a piece of paper 5x12cm (2x5in). Glue flowers onto it, as shown in step 6.

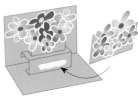

9. Glue the front of piece B. Press the flowery strip firmly onto it, and leave all the glue to dry.

Decorate a fancy envelope to put your card inside.

You could glue flowers on the front of the card too.

Paper roses

A bouquet of handmade roses is a long-lasting and less expensive alternative to real ones. Red traditionally stands for love, but you could also use pink, yellow or white paper.

You will need:

❀ red crêpe paper ❀ green crêpe paper ❀ florist's wire
❀ thin wire (e.g. from a hardware store) ❀ thread
❀ glue ❀ pencil ❀ scissors ❀ ruler

Long, folded edge

Short side

1. Cut out a 12x35cm (5x14in) strip of red tissue paper. Fold the long sides together.

2. Open it out and glue the lower half. Press the halves together, then let them dry.

3. With the long, folded edge nearest to you, fold the paper in half from left to right three times.

Don't cut the bottom edge.

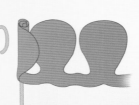

Thread

4. Draw a petal shape as shown here and cut around it. Carefully unfold it.

5. Bend one end of the florist's wire into a small loop. Roll the first two petals tightly around it.

6. Wrap the other petals less tightly, pinching them at the base. Tie with thread.

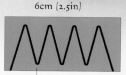

6cm (2.5in)

3cm (1in)

Don't cut too near the bottom.

7. To make sepals, which go beneath the petals, draw this pattern on the green paper and cut it out. Use the lower part.

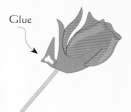

Glue

8. Put glue on the straight edge and wind it tightly around the base of the petals.

9. To make a leaf, cut out two leaf shapes like these. Glue them together with thin wire in the middle.

You'll need to repeat steps one to twelve for every rose that you make.

Long paper strip for stem

Leaf wires

10. Repeat step 9 to make another leaf. Put the two side by side and twist the wires together.

11. For the stem, cut a strip of paper 1.5cm (0.5in) wide. Glue one end to the sepals.

12. Twist the leaf wires onto the stem 4cm (1.5in) down. Wind the paper down over them.

Pressing flowers

Most flowers have short lives, but pressing them is a way to preserve them for longer. You can press leaves, too. Stick your flowers and leaves on a diary or notebook, or use them to decorate cards.

You will need:

❀ small, open-faced flowers ❀ leaves
❀ heavy books ❀ blotting paper ❀ tweezers

Pressed
verbenas

Selecting flowers

Choose clean, healthy blooms with no ugly marks. Look carefully at the edges of the petals and leaves to make sure they haven't been nibbled by bugs or slugs.

Press the flowers soon after picking them. Never pick wild flowers – there won't be any left for other people to enjoy. If you prefer, you could buy some flowers to press.

Pressed viola
flowers and
a fern leaf

Pick flowers
on a sunny
day, when
they're dry.

1. Use fresh flowers that have fully opened. Pick the flowerhead, along with a small length of stem.

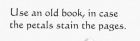
Use an old book, in case the petals stain the pages.

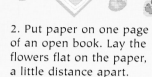

2. Put paper on one page of an open book. Lay the flowers flat on the paper, a little distance apart.

Look for flowers that are naturally flat, such as violas, petunias and primulas like these. Bulky flowers don't press as easily.

3. Lay another piece of paper over the flowers. Smooth it down gently, then close the book.

Protecting your flowers

Pressed flowers are very fragile and tear easily, so use tweezers to pick them up. Your flowers will fade or turn brown naturally over time, but if you keep them out of direct sunlight, they will stay brighter for longer.

With a little care, flowers will keep their looks for a long time after being pressed.

4. Stack more books on top. Leave the flowers in the book for at least two weeks to dry and flatten.

Using pressed flowers

You can use pressed flowers to decorate all kinds of things, such as cards, bookmarks and gift tags. Press them yourself (see page 172), or buy pre-pressed flowers from craft stores.

You will need:

❁ thin cardboard ❁ pressed flowers and leaves ❁ tweezers ❁ glue
❁ hole punch ❁ scissors ❁ clear book-covering film

1. Cut out shaped pieces of cardboard to make your gift tags and bookmarks.

2. Use tweezers to lay the flowers and leaves on the cardboard. Try out different arrangements.

3. Dab a dot of glue on the back of each flower and leaf, then stick them down.

Gift tags

To turn your cardboard shape into a gift tag, use the hole punch to make a hole in the top. Thread a ribbon through the hole to tie the tag to a gift.

Cut your gift tags in various shapes, such as hearts, circles and blossoms.

Bookmarks

Stick small, delicate flowers and leaves to strips of cardboard to make bookmarks. You can make the flowers last longer if you cover the front of the cardboard in clear book-covering film.

Cut the film sticky-side up.

Peel the backing from the film and lay it on the front of the bookmark. Smooth it out, turn it over, and cut around the edge.

Pressed rosebuds

Pretty pictures

Try arranging lots of one type of flower in a pattern, such as a circle or a ladder-like shape. You could also experiment with flowers and leaves to make a bouquet design.

You can print out templates for making bookmarks, gift tags and picture frames on the Usborne Quicklinks Website at www.usborne-quicklinks.com.

Tie some ribbon in a bow to decorate your bouquet.

Put your flower picture in a frame or cardboard mount.

Everlasting flowers

Flowers with small, stiff leaves or large seed pods can be dried to preserve their looks, sometimes for many years. This works because a flower can't rot when it's lost all its moisture.

You will need:

❀ assorted flowers ❀ rubber bands
❀ string ❀ scissors

Pick long-stemmed flowers, a little before they're fully open.

Dried statice, amaranthus and strawflowers

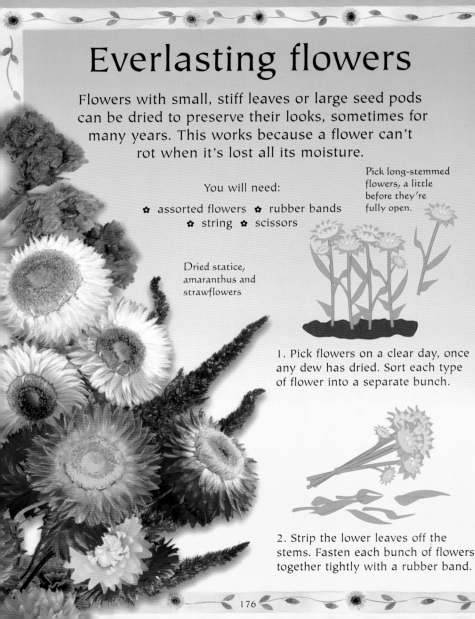

1. Pick flowers on a clear day, once any dew has dried. Sort each type of flower into a separate bunch.

2. Strip the lower leaves off the stems. Fasten each bunch of flowers together tightly with a rubber band.

Ears of corn

You could also try drying grasses, berries or seed pods. Some work better than others, so experiment with different things.

Berry sprig

Poppy seed heads

3. Fan the flower heads out a little so that they aren't touching each other. This stops them from rotting.

Keep the flowers hanging until the stems are completely stiff.

Dried flowers are delicate, so handle them carefully when you arrange them.

4. Hang the bunches from the string in a warm, airy place away from direct sunlight, such as a garage.

5. Display your dried flowers in a basket, jug or vase, so you can see the flowers but not the stems.

Lucky flowers

Some flowers are associated with a particular month
of the year. It's said that the flower of the month
you were born in will bring you good luck.

January: Snowdrop
Snowdrops are one of
the earliest flowers
to grow after the
cold of winter. For
this reason, they
symbolize hope.

February: Violet
Garlands of
violets used to be
given to children
for luck on their
third birthday.

March: Daffodil
Daffodils are a
traditional Easter
bloom, and also
the national
flower of Wales.

April: Sweet pea
The sweet pea is
commonly known as
the queen of annuals.

May: Lily of the Valley
In France, it's believed
that giving someone a lily
on the first day of May
will bring luck all year.

June: Rose
Roses are age-old symbols of
love and beauty. They're also
linked to royalty and religion.

July: Water lily or lotus

The lotus is a sacred flower in Hinduism and Buddhism, because it represents purity and perfection.

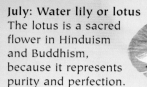

*

August: Gladiolus

The blade-like shape of its leaves inspired this flower's name, which means "sword" in Latin.

September: Morning glory

Morning glories take their name from the fact that they open in the morning. Each flower blooms for one day, then dies.

*

*

October: Cosmos

"Cosmos" means "orderly universe". This flower came to represent order because of its evenly spaced petals.

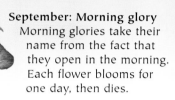

November: Chrysanthemum

Chrysanthemums are the national flower of Japan, where they represent both the Sun and life itself.

*

*

December: Holly

Ancient monks believed that holly could repel evil.

Flower language

In England, during Queen Victoria's reign, the "language of flowers" was a very popular idea. Giving a particular type of flower was a way of passing on a secret message to a friend or sweetheart.

Sharing feelings

In the 19th century, it was considered rude to talk openly about your feelings. Using flowers allowed people to express their emotions without speaking. Here are just a few of the hundreds of blooms that were given a meaning.

Cabbage flowers revealed that you would profit from something.

*

Rhododendrons were used to warn a lover of danger.

Star-of-Bethlehem flowers were a symbol of purity.

White stonecrop flowers represented calmness.

As you might think, forget-me-nots meant you wanted to be remembered.

A hidden code

When they wanted to share more complex thoughts, people exchanged small bouquets called tussie-mussies. Each different type of flower in the bouquet would form part of a secret message. So, the flowers shown on this page mean "Everyone agrees that you have beautiful eyes. I resolve to win you."

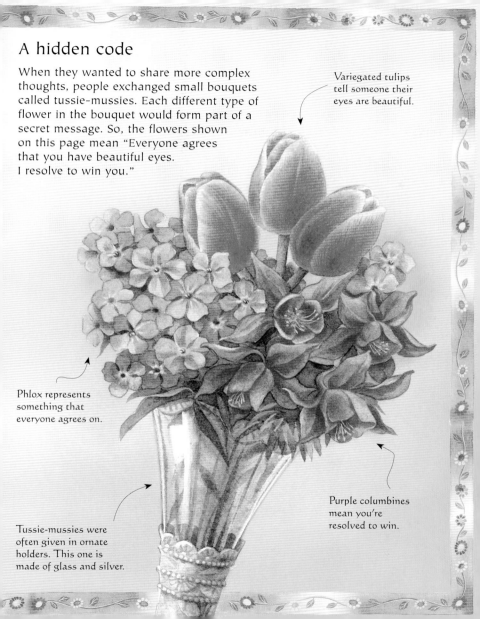

Variegated tulips tell someone their eyes are beautiful.

Phlox represents something that everyone agrees on.

Purple columbines mean you're resolved to win.

Tussie-mussies were often given in ornate holders. This one is made of glass and silver.

Myths and legends

Many flowers take their names from ancient stories which explain how they came to exist, or why they look or grow the way they do.

Lady slippers

The lady slipper orchid's name comes from a Native American story. A young girl went to fetch medicine when the people of her village developed a terrible disease, but along the way, she lost her shoes in a blizzard. Although her feet were frozen and bleeding, she struggled on. Her courage saved the village, and, when the snow melted, shoe-shaped flowers bloomed in her footprints.

The lady slipper's spots are said to represent blood from the brave little girl's feet.

A Christmas tale

The legend of the Christmas rose begins at the birth of Jesus. When a shepherd girl cried at having no gift to give to the baby, an angel turned her tears into a bouquet of delicate white flowers.

Christmas roses bloom at Christmas time.

Greek myths

Iris flowers are named after the Greek goddess of the rainbow. Iris was said to have painted the sky with her rainbow, and crossed it to carry messages from heaven to Earth. Irises grew wherever her feet touched the ground.

*

The name "iris" literally means "eye of heaven".

Yarrow is also known as Achillea, after an ancient Greek hero named Achilles. It was said that he gave this plant to his soldiers to heal their wounds. Modern tests show that yarrow really does contain chemicals that stop blood from flowing.

Yarrow

According to an ancient Greek tale, Narcissus was the most handsome man in the world. He drowned while trying to kiss his reflection in a lake, but the gods turned him into a flower so his beauty would live on after his death.

Wild asters take their name from the Greek goddess Asterea. Legend has it that when she looked down on the Earth and saw no stars in the sky, her tears of sadness turned into star-shaped flowers.

"Aster" is the Latin word for "star".

Narcissus

Flower superstitions

People used to think that flowers could influence their future, bring good or bad luck and protect them from harm. Superstitions like these are found all over the world.

Arum lily

Rosemary planted by a door was thought to strengthen friendship.

Rosemary

Arum lilies, sometimes called death lilies, had a strange double meaning. In a bride's bouquet they were seen as lucky, but a bouquet of them in your home was said to invite death.

Farmers hung primroses in their cowsheds to stop fairies from stealing the milk.

Bad luck was believed to follow if all the petals fell from a freshly cut rose.

Rose

Snapdragon

Snapdragons were said to keep people safe from curses.

Primrose

Monkshood was believed to repel werewolves.

Monkshood is also known as wolfsbane.

It was once thought that if you cut a sunflower while making a wish, your wish would come true before the next sunset.

Sunflower

Another name for a viola is heart's-ease.

People used to think that violas could cure a broken heart, because their petals are heart-shaped.

Legend has it that adding cuckoo flowers to a May garland would bring the wearer bad luck, or even cause them to be carried away to Fairyland.

Cuckoo flowers

Daisy

Daisies are used in a traditional game to discover someone's feelings. The petals are picked one by one, while saying "loves me... loves me not". The last petal reveals if you are loved, or not.

Dreaming about daisies was thought to be lucky in spring or summer, but unlucky in autumn or winter.

Useful flowers

Flowers and plants that have a practical use are called herbs. In the past, most people grew their own herbs and used them to make food, drinks and medicines.

Herbal medicine

Before the 19th century, almost all diseases were treated using parts of plants. Many traditional remedies have been forgotten or are no longer thought to work, but others are still widely used.

* St John's Wort has been used through the ages to ease depression.

* People used to believe that drinking a potion of daisy juice for fifteen days cured insanity.

Although some ancient herbal remedies are based on superstition, there's no doubt that flowers can be used to make medicine. In fact, around a quarter of all modern drugs prescribed by doctors come from plants.

Foxgloves are the source of digitalis, a drug used to treat heart disease.

Kitchen herbs

Cooks have used the mouthwatering smell and taste of herbs for many centuries. Although the parts of the plant that are used today are mostly the leaves or roots, some types of flowers can safely be eaten too.

Nasturtium leaves and petals can be added to salads for a peppery taste.

Dried clove flower buds are used as a spice, often in cooked fruit dishes.

Spice it up

Spices are herbs with a particularly strong taste or smell. Many spices, such as nutmeg and vanilla, are made from a flower's seeds or seed pods.

Sweet dreams

Lavender is a herb whose scent brings peaceful sleep. Try making these decorative lavender bags and keeping them by your pillow.

You will need:

❀ dried lavender ❀ ribbon ❀ chalk
❀ scissors ❀ fabric ❀ a plate

You can buy dried lavender in health food stores, or dry some yourself.

Tie the ribbon into a bow.

Fabric circle

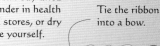

1. Draw around the plate with the chalk to make a circle. Cut it out.

2. Put a handful of lavender in the middle. Bunch up the fabric over the top.

3. Tightly tie a ribbon around the fabric to hold it together.

Sweet scents

The scent of a flower comes from oils in its petals.
This aroma has an important purpose in nature, and
people have many uses for fragrant flowers too.

Why do flowers smell?

In the natural world, flowers have
scent to attract pollen-carriers. Many
scented flowers have unpatterned
petals, because they
don't need bright
markings to lure
insects in.

Orange blossoms look
plain but smell luscious.

Not all flowers smell good – some
appeal to insects because they
smell of rotten meat or bad eggs.

A stapelia's
foul stink
attracts flies to
carry its pollen.

Scentless flowers

Some flowers don't need to attract
insects, so they have
no scent at all.

Ribwort plantain is
pollinated by the wind,
so it has no scent.

The history of perfume

The ancient Egyptians were the first
people known to make perfume
from flowers. They soaked their skin
in flower oils, and kept themselves
smelling attractive by melting cones of
animal fat and petals on their heads.

This ancient Egyptian painting shows women
wearing flower-scented cones in their hair.

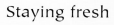

Scenting the home

People use flowers to scent their homes as well as their bodies. In the past, they did this by scattering fresh herbs on the floor, which released their scent when crushed underfoot. Today, displays of dried or fresh flowers have the same purpose, but can be decorative too.

Staying fresh

Before cities had sewers, floral perfumes disguised the smell of dirty streets and homes, as well as smelly clothes. In the 18th century, rich people often walked around with balls of beeswax and petals called pomanders held under their noses, or carried on their sleeves.

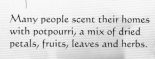

Many people scent their homes with potpourri, a mix of dried petals, fruits, leaves and herbs.

Making perfume

The simplest way to extract oil from petals involves boiling flowers and water. The mix gives out steam, which cools and becomes drops of water and flower oil. These can then be separated. A huge number of flowers is needed to obtain just a little oil, so the floral scents in most perfumes are made artificially.

Only the most expensive fragrances contain pure flower oils.

Amazing but true

The biggest...
The world's largest flower is the rafflesia, which can reach up to 1m (3ft) across. It grows on tropical vines, stealing their food and water.

A rafflesia flower has thick, fleshy petals, but no leaves, stem or roots.

...and smallest
The smallest flowers in the world belong to a group of water plants called wolffia. One dozen of them would fit on a pinhead.

Extended families
The largest families of flowering plants are the sunflower family, with over 24,000 species, and the orchid family, with 20,000 species.

Orchids come in thousands of varieties.

*

Busy bees
Honey bees must gather nectar from two million flowers to make 500g (1lb) of honey.

Honey bees

Costly spice
The most expensive spice in the world is saffron. 250,000 crocus flower stamens are needed to make 500g (1lb) of it.

Crocus

Fascinating names
Peonies are one of the most highly valued flowers in the Far East. Their Chinese name is "sho yu", which means "most beautiful".

In Mexico, zinnias were originally called "mal de ojos", meaning "bad to the eyes". The flowers were thought of as small and ugly.

Zinnias

Blossom watching
Every April in Japan, people sit under cherry trees to watch the falling pink blossoms. This tradition is called "O-hanami" or "flower viewing". It's believed that good energy flows from the tree to the people sitting beneath.

Sticky solutions
In the 16th century, a liquid found in bluebell roots and bulbs was commonly used to glue pages into books.

Flower dye
The chemical that gives marigolds their bright orange petals can be used to dye clothes and hair.

Marigolds *

Floral soap
The soapwort flower takes its name from the fact that its leaves produce a soapy lather when rubbed.

Soapwort was once used as soap.

Seed stuffing
Milkweed seeds are attached to hairs that are so lightweight, they were originally used to stuff lifejackets.

Milkweed seeds

A late developer
The rare Puya raimondii plant doesn't flower until it's 150 years old. After that, it dies.

Rare types of tulip bulbs were once sold for their own weight in gold.

Tulipmania
During the 17th century, "tulipmania" swept Holland. Tulips were so valuable that certain types were used as money, with their value changing daily.

Masters of disguise
Stone plants look like small pebbles, which stops hungry animals from eating them.

Stone plants

Fruity flowers

Fig flowers grow inside the fruits. Each fruit has a tiny opening in the top, so that pollinating insects can reach the flowers.

Fig flowers

Popping out

Some types of evening primrose flowers unfurl so quickly that they burst open, making a popping sound.

What, no petals?

Eucalyptus flowers have no petals. The parts that show are the stamens.

Eucalyptus stamens

Central heating

As Alpine snowbells sprout high up in the Swiss Alps, their shoots produce enough heat to melt holes in the winter snow. They can then reach the surface to flower in early spring.

Alpine snowbells

Ancient collectors

The first recorded plant collectors were soldiers in the army of Tuthmosis III, Pharaoh of Egypt 3,500 years ago. Carvings in the Temple of Karnak show them bringing back hundreds of plants from military campaigns in Syria.

Turning around

When growing around a support, most climbing plants twist in a clockwise spiral. But greater bindweed can only turn anti-clockwise. If it's forced to twine the other way, it will eventually die.

Greater bindweed

Toxic flower

Monkshood is one of the most poisonous flowering plants. Eating any part of it can cause serious illness or even death.

Monkshood

White water lily

Water holders

Rainforest bromeliads fill with rainwater. The largest can hold up to 54 litres (12 gallons) of water. These pools provide homes for hundreds of water insects and tiny frogs.

Bromeliad

Sinking flowers

During the day, white water lily flowers float on the surface of ponds but, at night, the flowers close and sometimes sink below the surface until morning.

Bleeding roots

Bloody crane's-bill gets its name from the blood red sap that seeps from its roots when it's damaged. The crane's-bill part comes from its long, pointed fruit which look like the beak of a crane – a long-necked, long-legged wading bird.

Marvellous medicine

Rosy periwinkles contain a chemical that fights some types of cancer.

Rosy periwinkle

Sprouting trunks

Many rainforest trees, such as durian and cacao, have flowers that grow directly from their trunks.

Arum

Arum fly trap

Arum flowers catch flies in a ring of hairs inside their flowerheads. As they struggle, the flies drop pollen onto the flower's ovaries. Their job done, the hairs wither, and the flies escape.

Seashore

Beside the seaside

Shores and coasts are where the sea meets the land. From craggy cliffs to golden beaches, they are excellent places to explore and hunt for unique wildlife.

Homes for all

Wind, salt spray and lack of shelter can make life by the sea challenging, but many plants and animals are suited to it. Every coastal landscape, from mud to rocks, offers some living thing the conditions it needs for survival.

Gulls are one of the few animals that can be found on all types of shores.

Sandy shores

People usually visit sandy beaches to relax in the sun. Sunlight is less appealing to many shore animals, though, as too much of it dries out their fragile bodies. The creatures that live here are mostly hidden away under the sand, or beneath rocks.

Although this beach looks empty of life, hundreds of worms and shelled animals could be buried in the sand.

Rocky shores

Despite being one of the harshest seashore environments, rocky coasts are home to a marvellous mixture of animals and plants. In fact, the pools of water left between the rocks are mini sea worlds by themselves.

Anemones in pools look like flowers, but they're really meat-eating animals.

Tiny fish dart through the water.

Starfish

Some plants and animals stick to rocks to keep from being washed away.

Muddy shores

Mudflats form where fresh water from rivers meets salty sea water. The dirt and sand they contain sticks together to make thick mud. Thousands of birds fly in from other countries to find food on mudflats.

Looking for treasure

Besides animals, there are lots of interesting things to spot on the shore, such as fossils and shells. Even on an empty beach, you can examine towering cliffs, or watch the mesmerizing motion of the waves.

This spongy mass used to contain a sea creature's eggs.

Birds with long beaks probe in mud for slimy creatures to eat.

Exploring the shore

Scientists divide the shore into several zones, which are based on how much and how often the sea covers the ground. You can identify each one by what lives there.

The tides

Twice a day, the tide comes in and goes out. When the beach is mostly covered it's high tide, and when the sea's far away, it's low tide. The tides create the zones.

High tide reaches here.

Low tide usually falls here.

Splash zone

Upper zone   Middle zone   Lower zone   *

Splash zone

This bit of the shore is furthest from the sea. The few animals and plants that live here are sprayed by the tide when it's in, but never covered.

Upper zone

The tide leaves parts of this zone exposed for days at a time. Animals that live here usually have shells to retreat into for safety until the sea covers them again.

Washed-up channelled wrack

Thrift

Most of the upper zone's inhabitants are shelled creatures called barnacles.

Rough periwinkle

Lichens are plants which grow on stones in the splash zone.

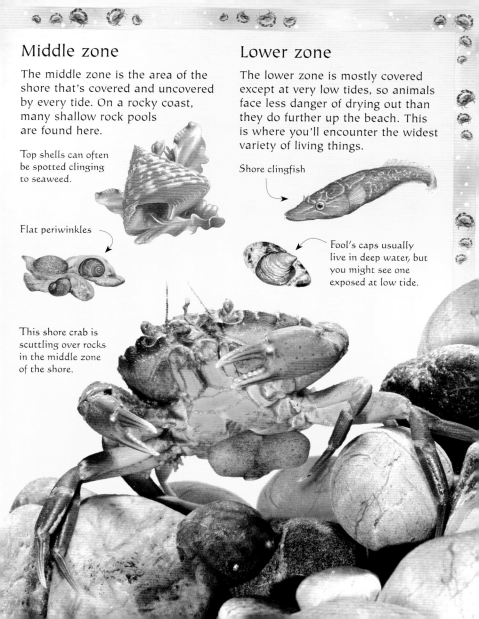

Middle zone

The middle zone is the area of the shore that's covered and uncovered by every tide. On a rocky coast, many shallow rock pools are found here.

Top shells can often be spotted clinging to seaweed.

Flat periwinkles

This shore crab is scuttling over rocks in the middle zone of the shore.

Lower zone

The lower zone is mostly covered except at very low tides, so animals face less danger of drying out than they do further up the beach. This is where you'll encounter the widest variety of living things.

Shore clingfish

Fool's caps usually live in deep water, but you might see one exposed at low tide.

Tough plants

Life is much tougher for a coastal plant than its inland relatives. Growing on the shore means having to survive against salt spray, strong winds and unsteady ground.

A constant struggle

Seashore plants tend to have special shapes or features that allow them to endure the harsh coastal climate, so look closely to spot them. For instance, some have thick, waxy leaves, which keep them from drying out in the wind.

Yellow horned poppies gather fresh rainwater on their fuzzy leaves.

Sea holly, like its inland relative, has tough, hard leaves.

Although plants aren't as widespread around the coast as they are inland, every area has different kinds for you to find.

Marram grass leaves roll into narrow tubes in dry weather, trapping damp air inside.

The few trees that grow near the sea often twist into dramatic and permanent windswept shapes, like this one.

On shingle beaches

Shingle beaches are made of stones and shells with a little sand mixed in. The shingle is constantly shifted by the tides, meaning only plants with deep roots can survive.

Shrubby seablite

Sea bindweed

Sea kale

*

On salt marshes

Old mudflats which are now covered in plants are called salt marshes. They're regularly engulfed by the tide, so plants that live there have to be able to deal with salt water. In fact, some have adapted so well that they can't grow without it.

Sea lavender

*

Sea spurrey

Sea aster

On cliffs

Plants struggle hard to grow on cliffs. Most cliff plants have low, bushy shapes so their stems aren't snapped by the fierce winds. Their long roots also creep into cracks in rocks, anchoring them firmly in place.

Sea campion

Golden samphire

Sand dune life

Dunes are large mounds of sand which build up
when winds whirl around grasses far up the beach.
They're home to many different kinds of wildlife.

How sand dunes form

Sea lyme
grass

Sea couch
grass

Marram
grass

*

Wind

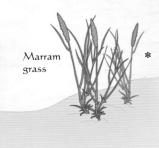

1. The wind blows
dry sand up from the
beach. It gathers in low
ridges around grasses
near the high tide line.

2. More ridges build up
around grasses beyond
the high tide line. The
growing sand pile is
called a fore dune.

3. Marram grass grows
all over the sand pile,
which keeps growing.
Its long roots stop the
dune from breaking up.

Dune plants

When the dune is big and strong, other
plants besides grasses start to grow on
it. Most of them have creeping stems,
tough leaves and small flowers. Here
are some types to look out for.

Sea rocket

Viper's
bugloss

Bird's foot
trefoil

Sea sandwort

Animals to spot

As well as plants, sand dunes are home to lots of creepy crawlies, furry creatures and even rare toads and reptiles.

Rabbits are good for sand dunes, because their droppings help plants grow.

Foxes hunt for rabbits and may even move into their abandoned burrows.

*

Many moths and butterflies live on dunes.

Small pools of water between dunes are occasionally home to natterjack toads. Their skin gives out a nasty rubbery smell.

Dunes in danger

A growing dune is very fragile. If large gaps start to appear between the grasses, wind blows through and scatters the sand until the whole dune breaks up, leaving the animals that live there without a home. You can help preserve dunes by never digging in them or pulling out plants.

Without dunes to live on, endangered sand lizards like this would die out.

Wonderful weeds

Whether it's waving gracefully in the water, drying on the beach in the sun or slicked over rocks, you rarely have to look far on the seashore to find seaweed.

What is seaweed?

Seaweed belongs to a group of plants called algae, with no roots, leaves or flowers. It mostly grows under water, but often gets washed ashore by the sea. Some kinds stay moist on land, while others crackle up.

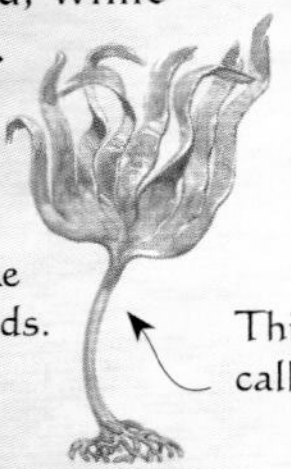

Bladder wrack

*

These leaf-like parts are fronds.

Thick stalk, called a stipe

This thick vein running up the middle of a frond is called a midrib.

Weed versus waves

Although it's constantly pulled about by the sea, seaweed is up to the challenge. Pods called air bladders in its fronds keep it upright in the water, and sucker-like holdfasts firmly stick it to rocks so it doesn't get swept away.

Disc-shaped

See if you can spot all the types of holdfasts shown here.

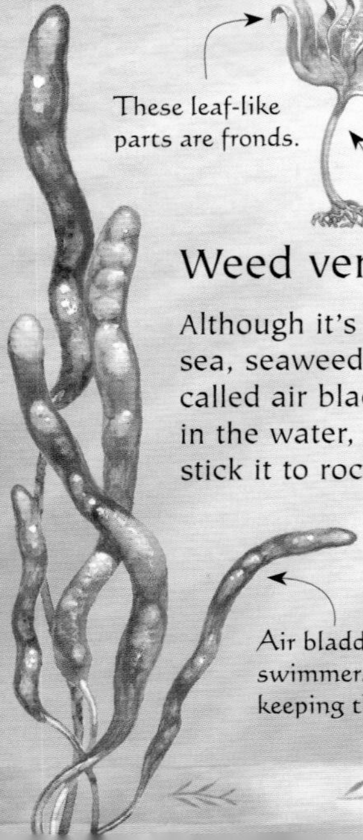

Air bladders act like swimmers' armbands, keeping the seaweed afloat.

Branched

Button-shaped

Types of seaweed

You may have noticed that seaweed comes in three different colours – green, red, and brown, like the knotted wrack below. All three kinds can be seen on most shores, although you'll need to look in different areas to find them.

Green seaweeds, like this sea lettuce, grow in the upper and middle zones.

Red seaweeds are usually small. They live in rock pools and shallow water.

A closer look

Even a quick search on a beach reveals seaweed in many shapes and sizes. You might even notice other things living on the fronds. See how many kinds you can spot, and if anything is attached.

The white marks on this saw wrack are tiny tubes with worms inside.

Tangle has many thin, flat "fingers".

Tufts of red seaweed on knotted wrack

Hornwrack appears to be seaweed, but it's not. It's clusters of very small sea creatures.

Weather forecasting

It's said that a type of seaweed called sea belt can predict the weather. If you find a piece that's limp and moist, rain is coming. But if it's crispy, the weather will be fine.

Sea belt looks like a piece of ribbon with wavy edges.

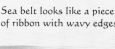

Plant or animal?

The seashore is so full of peculiar wildlife that it's sometimes hard to tell exactly what's what. All the things on these pages are animals, although they look like plants.

Anemones

Anemones live firmly attached to hard surfaces. When the tide is out they look like glistening pods, but under water they open up into vicious predators with poisonous tentacles.

Beadlet anemone *

These anemones have attached themselves to a crab. *

To catch their dinner, anemones wait until a small animal swims near.

The tentacles sting their prey and pull it into the anemone's gaping mouth.

Corals

Corals are made of many tiny animals called polyps. They can be entirely soft, or have hard skeletons outside their bodies. These skeletons join into groups known as colonies, which in turn form enormous coral reefs.

The gruesomely named dead man's fingers coral grows off shore. You might find it washed up on the beach after a storm.

Sea fan

Little fish live among corals.

Brain coral

Elkhorn coral

Sea sponges

Sponges grow all over the world, on the seabed or on rocks in the lower zone. Each one is actually lots of microscopic creatures inside a squishy outer "skeleton". People use the empty skeletons as natural bath sponges.

Purse sponge often grows on seaweed.

Mermaid's gloves have openings that regularly squirt out water.

Sea oranges are found in shallow water.

Waste water squirts out of the holes in these flowery shapes.

Little squirts

Sea squirts are very strange. The babies, which look like tadpoles, swim through the sea looking for a hard surface to stick to. They then grow into jelly-like adults, as shown above.

Animals in disguise

A few sea creatures have bodies that are specially adapted to fool other animals into thinking they are plants. This allows them to hide from enemies, or sneak up on prey.

This is a sea dragon. It's a type of fish, but it looks more like seaweed.

Prickles and poison

Headless creatures with poisonous spikes and the ability to clone themselves sound like something from a science fiction movie, but they actually exist on the seashore.

Living cucumbers

Despite their name, sea cucumbers are animals, not vegetables. When threatened, they spurt strings of sticky (and sometimes poisonous) guts all over an opponent. The cucumber escapes, and new guts grow back in a few weeks.

Sea cucumbers spray guts from their back ends all over an enemy.

A ball of thorns

Sea urchins are not to be messed with. Their hard, round bodies are covered with many sharp, moveable spikes, each one loaded with poison. The urchin's mouth, on the underside of its body, is filled with razor-sharp teeth.

*

After an urchin dies, its spikes fall off. All that's left is its skeleton, which is called a test.

An urchin moves around using suckers called tube feet that sprout from between its spikes.

Sea potatoes are a type of urchin. Their small spines look like a coat of fur.

Stars of the ocean

Starfish and their close relatives, brittle stars, have bodies made of several arms joined at the centre. If an arm is broken off, the starfish will grow a new one and, amazingly, the detached arm might also grow into a new starfish.

Like an urchin, a starfish has spikes on its body, although they look more like little bumps.

A cushion star's dull body and small size make it hard to spot.

A brittle star can sacrifice an arm to escape from danger – in this case, a hungry flatfish.

Deadly diners

If you spot a starfish on top of a shellfish, it might be feeding. The starfish uses powerful suckers on its arms to prise the shell open a little, then turns its stomach inside-out to reach inside and digest its victim.

This starfish is using its suckered arms to wrestle open a shell.

Scales and fins

Many types of fish live, feed and breed around the shore.
Their range of body shapes and colours makes some
very obvious, but others can be trickier to spot.

Finding fish

A lot of fish live far out at sea, although
you'll still see quite a few if you stay
around rock pools, estuaries, bays
or any shallow water. Some fish
live on their own, and others
swim in groups called shoals.

A lumpsucker uses
this sucker on its belly
to anchor itself to rocks.

Sand smelts are usually
seen swimming in shoals
near the water's surface.

Flatfish like this dab
hide in sand on the
seabed. Their colour
allows them to blend in.

Fish food

Despite having no teeth, many fish feed on
other animals, swallowing worms or sucking
molluscs right out of their shells. You might
also spot them nibbling plants or poking
around for tiny creatures in mud and sand.

A corkwing wrasse crushes shelled
creatures between its thick lips.

Eggs to fry

Almost all fish lay eggs, which hatch into tiny babies called fry. Sometimes, one or both of the parents protects the eggs until they hatch. Look out for eggs stuck on weeds, and colourful male fish showing off to plainer females before they mate.

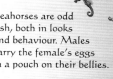

Hatching babies

Seahorses are odd fish, both in looks and behaviour. Males carry the female's eggs in a pouch on their bellies.

*

Female tompot blennies lay eggs in rocky crevices.

A rainbow wrasse starts life as a dull brown female, then changes into a bright male as it grows up.

*

Female wrasse

Male wrasse

Self defence

Fish are eaten by larger animals, so they need to be able to protect themselves. They usually hide in seaweeds or sand, but some can change colour to match the scenery. A few types deter foes with poison.

This scorpion fish's patterned body warns enemies, "Don't eat me, I'm poisonous!"

A worm pipefish can easily hide among thin seaweeds.

Body armour

Some creatures that live on the seashore have several legs, and hard body coverings to protect them from greedy enemies. These creatures are crustaceans.

Crusty crabs

Crabs are a common sight on most shores, scuttling sideways with their claws held high to frighten away attackers. The smallest crabs are barely bigger than a pea, but the largest, the Japanese spider crab, grows up to 3.7m (12ft) wide.

An edible crab's shell has a wavy edge that looks like pastry crust.

*

Most crabs have eight legs and two claws.

Thornback spider crabs have hairy-looking shells.

Getting undressed

Most crabs shed their shells once in a while to let their bodies expand, then grow a new one. Hermit crabs are different. They grow hard coverings on their front parts and use another animal's empty shell to protect their soft rear.

This hermit crab has just found itself a new suit of armour.

Lurking lobsters

Lobsters are shy beasts that like to lurk in secret hideaways, so the best place to look for one is a rocky crevice or hole. You can recognize them by their jointed bodies, long feelers and huge claws. Many people think lobsters are red, but in fact most are blue or green.

Lobsters have fan-shaped tails. Here, it's tucked under the body.

The large claw cracks open shells and the smaller one tears meat.

Sensitive feelers

Shrimps and prawns

Prawns and similar many-legged crustaceans swim around in shallow sea water and rock pools, waving their long feelers around to detect food.

Shrimps are almost see-through in water.

A chameleon prawn can change colour to hide itself.

Beach hoppers look a little like jumping woodlice.

Sticking around

Unlike other crustaceans, barnacles don't move. They glue their bodies to a hard surface, forming a dome with their armour. To feed, they unfurl their feathery legs through a narrow hatch in the top of the dome.

When they're under water, barnacles flick out their legs to catch prey.

Seashells

Walk along almost any beach and you'll find empty shells, the former homes of living things. If you're lucky, you might even see one complete with its slimy owner.

Animals with shells

Many animals have shells, but the type you're most likely to see on the shore are molluscs. These include snails, oysters and squid. Most molluscs – though not all – have their shells outside their bodies.

A squid's shell, called a pen, is inside its body.

This murex shell used to have an animal inside.

A pen looks like this.

Single shells

All the molluscs that live in the sea have either a single shell or two shells hinged together. Single-shelled sea creatures belong to the same family of animals as garden snails, and are known as gastropods.

A pelican's foot has a growth on its shell shaped like the bird's webbed toes.

Slipper limpets are often found on top of one another in chains of up to nine shells.

Double shells

Creatures called bivalves have two shells that are joined at a hinge, and which open and close like a book. Bivalves can move around surprisingly well, burrowing or, in a few cases, swimming away from danger.

In the water, scallops can swim away from enemies by clapping their two shells together.

This cockle isn't poking out its tongue. It uses this muscular foot to drag itself along the beach.

Mussels ooze out glue so they can stick to rocks.

Sea food

Molluscs come in both meat and plant-eating varieties. Gastropods use their saw-like tongues to scrape plants off rocks, or to drill holes in other animals' shells and eat their soft bodies. Many bivalves suck tiny living things called plankton out of the sea.

This meat-eating dog whelk is stretching out its sensitive feelers to detect a victim among the stones.

Blue-rayed limpets stick to the oarweed that they feed on.

In real life, these plankton are too small to see. There are countless numbers in the sea.

Birds on the beach

Muddy shores and quiet beaches are good places for birdwatching. When the tide goes out, it leaves behind hundreds of the tiny creatures that birds feed on.

Wading in

Waders are birds that spend most of their time feeding in sand or muddy water. The best place to see them is an estuary (a place where a river meets the sea). Mud can be dangerous, so don't try to get too close.

*

Black-headed gulls stomp on sand to lure worms to the surface.

Turnstones lift up pebbles to find shelled animals.

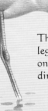

This avocet's long legs allow it to walk on wet ground without dirtying its feathers.

Sanderlings dart along the shore looking for shrimps and molluscs.

Wader watching

Most waders live in one country for part of the year, then fly to another to breed – sometimes as far away as Antarctica. April and September are the times of year when you're most likely to spot flocks of birds on their travels.

Hundreds of thousands of bar-tailed godwits visit Britain's coasts in winter.

Feeding together

Every type of bird on the shore eats different things, which means that lots of species can feed together peacefully on the same beach. A handy clue to what a bird eats is the shape of its beak.

Curlews use their slim, curved beaks to probe for tiny buried creatures.

Look for rows of little holes left behind in the sand by a dunlin's jabbing beak.

This oystercatcher has a long, strong beak for smashing mussel shells.

Nests and babies

Waders lay their eggs on beaches or grassy fields. Some build nests and others just scrape a hollow in the ground. This leaves the eggs and chicks wide open to attack, but they're hard to spot among the rocks and sand.

*

Little ringed plover eggs have a pattern which helps them blend into the shingle.

Clifftop birds

The rocky cliff faces that rise up along coasts might seem like dangerous places to live, yet they suit some types of birds perfectly.

Cliff bird features

Most cliff birds belong to one of three different bird families: auks, gulls and terns. These types of birds tend to be quite large, with black and white feathers and harsh, squawking calls. They also have webbed feet to help them swim.

Puffins are auks. They are agile swimmers, but awkward on land.

Herring gull

Gulls are a common sight on almost every shore.

Terns have forked tails and slim, sharp beaks.

Great black-backed gull

Fulmars spend hours gliding over the sea.

Soaring seabirds

When the wind blows in from the sea and cliffs block its path, the only way it can go is up. Birds stretch their wings and glide on this rising air. Gliding uses much less energy than flapping, allowing them to stay aloft longer and look for food further afield.

Catch of the day

Almost all birds that live on cliffs catch fish. Some hover over the water in one spot, dropping suddenly to catch the fish unawares. Others skim lightly over the water's surface, or go diving and catch their dinner beneath the waves.

Manx shearwaters almost touch, or "shear", the sea with their wing tips.

*

Razorbills can grab several fish in one go.

Storm petrels flutter over the sea at night, to avoid enemies.

Gannets dive from spectacular heights to catch fish. Look for their bright yellow heads.

*

Cliff safety

Always take care around cliffs – don't try to climb them or go near the edge, and never disturb a bird's nesting site. The safest way to look at seabirds on clifftops is from a distance, through binoculars.

Kittiwakes are small gulls with black legs. This one is on a cliff, but you might also see them on coastal buildings or piers.

Finding a partner

Like all birds, seashore birds pair up to mate and have babies. First, the birds have to impress each other with fancy displays. This is called courtship. Most couples stay together their whole lives after courtship has taken place.

Before mating, black-headed gulls run side-by-side with their heads down.

*

*

The male gull also coughs up food as a gift for the female.

Cliff colonies

There are few trees and bushes near the coast, so cliff birds build their nests on rocks, cliffs and islands. Some live in groups of a thousand or more, each one nesting just out of pecking distance of the others. A few birds, such as puffins, dig burrows to house their eggs.

Gannets nest in huge flocks. The same couples return to the same rocky islands to breed every year.

Shags make their nests out of twigs and seaweed.

Nestless wonders

Surprisingly, some cliff birds don't make a home for their eggs at all. Instead, they lay them directly on the rocks. Since a fall would shatter them, the eggs are specially shaped so they can't roll away.

Guillemots lay a single pear-shaped egg on a ledge. Its shape makes it roll in circles, not off the cliff edge.

Growing up

Baby cliff birds emerge from their eggs into a dangerous world of chilling winds and hungry enemies. Luckily, they have fluffy feathers to keep them warm and make them hard to see. These are replaced by smooth ones as the chick grows.

Although this herring gull chick is in plain view on the top of a cliff, its brown feathers fool enemies into thinking it's a stone.

The chick will one day have snowy white feathers and a colourful beak, like its parent.

Animal hide and seek

Beaches sometimes appear to have no life on them
at all, but looks can be deceiving. Many seashore
animals are very good at hiding themselves.

Buried beasts

Some sea creatures are very efficient
diggers, burrowing down into the
sand at top speed to avoid danger.
When the tide is out, they burrow
deeper to find moisture. Most
of these diggers are found
on the lower shore.

This masked crab is
visiting the surface.
It normally lives in
the sand.

Watch for sand
eels disappearing
down into the sand
near to the sea.

In the mud

Creatures that live in mud move around
less than sand-dwellers, and tend to
live deeper down. Their bodies have
long tubes that reach to the surface
for feeding and removing waste.

If you were to dig
deep on a muddy
beach, you might
find these shells.

Peppery
furrow shell

Common
otter shell

Blunt
gaper

Signs in the sand

You probably won't have much luck finding buried creatures if you dig randomly in the sand or mud. The secret to finding them lies on the surface, where they leave hints to their location. You'll have to dig fast to see the animals before they burrow away.

Sea potatoes like this one leave paw-shaped imprints.

Casts are squiggly piles of sand that buried worms have squeezed out of their bodies.

It's not hard to guess what made this star-shaped mark.

When this razor shell buries itself, it leaves a hole with water squirting out.

Sand starfish

Wily worms

A number of worms are found on the shore, but you'll rarely see them on the surface. Like their relatives in gardens, they dig burrows in the ground or live under rocks, safe from peckish birds.

Look for ribbon worms under stones. They grow up to 50cm (20in) long.

Ribbon worm

A sea mouse is actually a worm that lives in the ocean. Its name refers to its furry-looking body.

Lugworm

Rare sightings

Some animals, such as gulls, are almost a guaranteed sight when you're on the shore. Others are much rarer or only live in certain places, but it's always worth being on the lookout.

Octopuses

Octopuses keep a low profile, making their homes in narrow, rocky crevices and only coming out at dusk and dawn to hunt. A pile of empty crab shells might be a sign of an octopus living nearby.

Common octopuses are actually much less common than the curled variety.

Look for a curled octopus like this one hiding in large rock pools.

*

Whales and dolphins

Dolphins are curious, friendly animals, so you might see them swimming alongside your boat if you go sailing. Whales are more often seen in the distance, rising up to blow water through holes in their heads.

*

Bottle-nosed dolphin

Porpoises are closely related to dolphins, but have smaller, blunt snouts.

A whale isn't a fish, it's a mammal, like you. Dolphins are mammals too.

Seals

Although seals aren't rare animals, they're hard to spot because they spend most of their time out at sea. The best time to see one is during the breeding season in June and July, when many gather on sandbanks.

Grey seals like this one live in small groups on remote, rocky shores.

Seals have short, sleek fur. A common seal's fur is always speckled.

The shark family

Despite their reputation for being huge man-eaters, sharks come in many sizes, and very few types attack people. Surfers sometimes encounter large sharks, but you're more likely to spot small ones like dogfish.

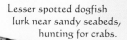

Thornback ray *

Lesser spotted dogfish lurk near sandy seabeds, hunting for crabs.

Rays are related to sharks. They swim by flapping their broad, wing-like fins.

Rock pools

Rock pools form wherever water gathers in hollows between stones and boulders on the shore. Many are teeming with life, making them a fascinating sight.

A shelter on the shore

Rock pools are very useful to many sea animals. When the tide's out, they're a refuge for creatures that need to stay wet. Deeper pools protect delicate animals that can't withstand pounding waves.

Low tide

High on the shore, rock pools are cut off from the sea when the tide is out. The animals are left to cope with salt, dry air and, in summer, fierce heat. Many creatures sit tight and wait for the sea to cover them again, while others hide or move.

*

Limpets stick firmly to the rocks.

Starfish crawl to the shelter of nearby seaweed clusters.

Blennies drag themselves from pool to pool using a pair of thin, stiff front fins.

Anemones stay moist when the tide's out by bunching up tightly into blobs.

*

High tide

A rock pool truly comes alive when the sea covers it at high tide. Fish take the chance to move to a new pool, anemones reach into the water to grab food, and slimy creatures slither over the rocks.

Breadcrumb sponges suck tiny morsels of food from the water.

Slippery butterfish squeeze between the rocks.

Seaweeds wave in the water, hiding little fish from hungry attackers.

Sea slugs crawl around looking for sponges to eat.

Things to remember

If you want to have a good look around a rock pool, it helps to be well prepared. To stay safe, always wear shoes with sturdy grips to avoid slipping on the wet rocks, and don't touch any animals – you might hurt them, or they might even hurt you. If you move a stone to look underneath, put it back afterwards. It could be an animal's home.

Rocks make great hiding places for small creatures.

Treasure hunting

Hunting for interesting animals or objects is a great way to spend a day on the shore. You might not find pirates' gold, but there are plenty of other treasures to discover.

Where to begin

A good place to start a treasure hunt is the strandline, the furthest point reached by the high tide. The sea leaves behind an intriguing hotch-potch of objects.

These glass pieces have been rubbed smooth by the waves.

Looking for life

Normally, you don't have to explore a beach for long before you find some sort of living thing. The strandline is an especially good place to spot creatures that have been brought ashore by the tide.

Beach hoppers leap around on rotting seaweed.

Portuguese men-of-war are related to corals. They can sting even when they wash up dead, so don't touch!

Look out for tiny long-clawed porcelain crabs. This one is actual size.

Animal signs

Even if you don't see many animals, you can search for things that they've left behind. Look closely and you could see anything from empty shells to feathers and bones.

Seabirds leave footprints in wet sand. A gull made this set.

Empty crab shells are pale on the inside.

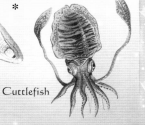

*

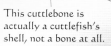

This cuttlebone is actually a cuttlefish's shell, not a bone at all.

Cuttlefish

Eggs and egg cases

Many types of sea creatures, including molluscs and fish, lay eggs. Most of these eggs come in strangely shaped soft cases, which you might spot on rocks and seaweed, or washed up on the sand.

This is an empty dogfish egg case, also known as a mermaid's purse.

Flat netted dog whelk cases are left in rows on eel grass.

Driftwood

Chunks of wood that have fallen into the sea and washed up on the shore are called driftwood. You might notice that they're unusually smooth, or have been bleached almost white by the salt water. Many are pocked with holes made by creepy crawlies.

Burrowing creatures called gribbles often leave behind holes in driftwood.

This driftwood's gnarled shape reflects the way trees grow around the coast.

Man-made objects

Some of the things you'll see on the strandline are just junk, like old cans and lollipop sticks. Look hard and you might find something more unusual, like an identification tag from a seal or seabird, or maybe a washed-up buoy.

People put tags and rings on animals so they can track their movements.

Buoys are usually tethered at sea, but can come loose.

Look out for tags like these on the beach.

Stones and shells

Even if you don't find anything else, it's still worth checking the strandline for distinctive shells and stones. Keep an eye out especially for odd shapes and colours, or patterns and stripes.

It's OK to look under seaweed stuck to rocks, but don't pull it off.

Pebble art

Seashore pebbles are ideal for decorating, because of their smooth surface. A little imagination can turn a pebble into a crab, a bug, a face, or anything you want it to be.

You will need:
⊛ smooth pebbles of different sizes
⊛ assorted acrylic paints
⊛ sheets of paper ⊛ a pencil
⊛ paintbrushes ⊛ clear varnish

Keep the pebbles on the paper as you work, to avoid stains.

1. Wash the pebbles. When they're dry, paint them white and leave the paint to dry.

2. Try out some designs on paper, then paint them onto your pebbles.

These pebbles have been painted with a seaside theme.

3. Leave the pebbles on some clean paper while the paint dries. Add a coat of varnish, if you like.

Seaside rocks

The shape of a rocky coastline and its cliffs, bays and pebbles tells a tale of the way time passes and the changes it brings to the landscape.

Tiny fragments

Most rocks found at the coast, like the ones shown here, start life inland. Rivers and streams wash dirt and mud into the sea, where they settle in layers. The bits, called sediment, are then squashed down by more layers of sediment above them, and gradually change into rock.

Limestone often has bits of shells mixed in with its sediment.

Chalk is a type of limestone. It's a soft, crumbly rock.

Hard and soft

Over hundreds of millions of years, rock builds up in layer upon layer. Some parts are very hard, while others are softer. The sea wears away the soft rocks easily, creating a bay, while cliffs are made when it breaks chunks off the hard parts.

The pounding waves wore this bay out of soft rock.

Arches and stacks

When bays develop along the coast, long strips of rock are sometimes left sticking out into the sea. These are known as headlands.

As more years pass, the sea might eventually batter the headland away too, carving out caves or impressive natural stone arches.

*

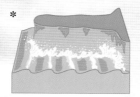

Waves hammer at all sides of the headland. Pieces of rock fall off.

After many hundreds of years, the water has worn the rock through.

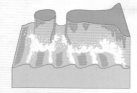

Eventually, the arch collapses and leaves behind a tower called a stack.

Pebbles on the beach

The largest lumps of rock that fall from a cliff or headland stay where they fall, but small ones get rubbed together in the sea, becoming smooth pebbles. A pebble's shape can give you a clue to the sort of rock it is.

Pebbles with coloured bands came from finely layered rocks.

*

The constant rolling of the tide sometimes creates cigar-shaped quartzite pebbles.

Many pebbles of sandstone, a sedimentary rock, are oval.

Hard granite often forms into ball-shaped pebbles.

Flat pebbles are often made of a rock called schist.

Sandy shores

Sand is what's left of rocks after millions of years
of wear and tear. Pick up a handful and you could
be touching something a dinosaur once walked on.

How does sand form?

Sand is a mixture of tiny particles brought
to the coast by rivers, and rocks broken
from cliffs. Over time, the sea pounds
them into ever-smaller pieces
until they become fine bits.

These are the materials
that make up the sand
particles on most beaches.

A crystal
called quartz

A crystal
called feldspar

Rocks, such
as limestone
and shale

Sand sculptures

If you've ever made a
sandcastle, you'll know that
moist sand is excellent for
building. Some seaside towns
even hold sand-sculpting
contests to create all kinds of
large and elaborate displays.

The beaches of Brazil are famous
for amazing sculptures like this
one. Some take days to build.

Sand ornaments

When you leave the beach, try taking home a bag of sand and using it to make a long-lasting souvenir.

You will need:
❀ 400g (14oz) sand ❀ 200g (7oz) cornflour ❀ old spoon ❀ paper ❀ 250ml (8fl oz) water ❀ old pan

This three-part sea monster is displayed on blue paper.

1. Mix the ingredients into the saucepan. Stir them thoroughly over a low heat.

2. When the mix has thickened, take it off the heat. Leave it on some paper to cool.

3. While the mix is still soft, mould it into any shape you like. Then leave it to dry.

Types of sand

Not all sand is alike. Its texture and colour varies, depending on what's in it. Volcanic rock creates gritty black sand, while pure white beaches are finely ground-up coral.

Natural glass, called obsidian, can be found on volcanic beaches.

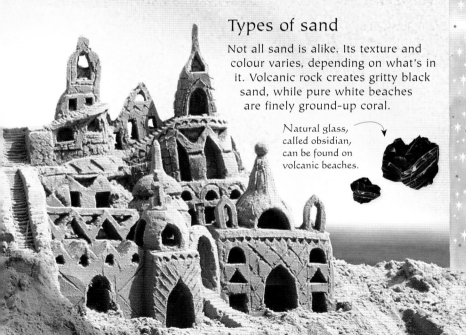

Wind and waves

The sea is never still. The wind whips it into waves and spray, while tides move it back and forth.

Sea breezes

You might have noticed it's breezy around the coast. This is because air moves from cool places to warm ones, and the sea and land are usually at different temperatures. Coastal winds can push sailboats along, and turn windmills to generate power.

Boats like this catch the wind in their sails.

Birth of a wave

When the wind blows over the ocean's surface, it creates ripples. Large ripples grow into peaks called crests, which start to travel faster and turn into waves. According to folklore, every seventh wave is more powerful than the others, but big waves are actually much less predictable.

Going nowhere

If you've ever seen a gull bobbing on the water, you may have wondered how it effortlessly stays in the same spot as waves pass by. It's because waves are just changes in the shape of the ocean's surface, so although they travel forwards, the water itself does not.

A surfer selects a single wave and rides it all the way to the shore.

Breaking waves

When a wave reaches the shore, its crest collapses and the wave is said to have broken. The shape of a breaking wave depends on how steeply the shore slopes into the water, so see if you can spot the difference.

The foam on top of a wave is called a whitecap.

*

In shallow water, the bottom of the wave drags on the ground. The top moves faster and breaks first.

Spilling breakers happen on gently sloping coasts. The waves break slowly, so the crest spills gently.

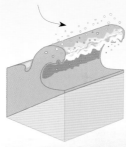

A plunging breaker occurs on steep shores. The waves curl completely over at the top and crash noisily down.

Building a beach

Waves are responsible for creating beaches. As they break on the shore and surge forwards, they leave behind lots of sediment. If enough remains when the water creeps back, a beach eventually builds up. The sea can carry sediment all along the coast when waves break at an angle to the shore.

Barriers called groynes are built to keep the moving sea from washing the sand away.

Fossil hunting

Beaches can be good places to go on a fossil hunt.
Finding fossils gives you a fascinating glimpse of
creatures that lived in the prehistoric world.

What is a fossil?

Fossils are the remains of ancient
living things. They're usually made
of an animal's hard parts, such
as its teeth, bones or shell,
but they can also be imprints
of things left behind in mud.

Fossilized
shark tooth

Millions of years
ago, this stone was soft
mud with a plant stuck in it.

Forming a fossil

These pictures show how a sea creature
called an ammonite becomes fossilized.

1. The ammonite
dies and sinks.
Its body rots,
leaving the shell.

2. Time passes.
Layers of sand
build up, burying
the shell deeper.

3. As centuries
pass, the shell is
broken down and
replaced by rock.

4. Eventually, a
shell-shaped rock
is left behind.
This is a fossil.

Seaside fossils

Most life from the past vanished without a trace, because plants and animals' soft bodies decayed over time. Sea creatures with hard shells, though, were perfect for fossilization. Some are ancestors of animals that roam the seas today.

Belemnites look like stone bullets, but they're the fossilized skeletons of squid-like creatures.

Trilobites lived over 245 million years ago, before dinosaurs existed.

*

*
Trilobite fossil in stone

Here's how a living belemnite might have looked.

Where to look

Not all shores are suitable for fossil hunting, although some are better than others. A beach surrounded by chalky cliffs is often a good place to start. There's more about where to look for fossils on the Usborne Quicklinks Website at www.usborne-quicklinks.com.

Limestone often contains fossilized shells, or imprints of their shapes.

You might find snail shell fossils embedded in rock, or – if you're lucky – on their own.

This is a fossilized sea urchin's skeleton. The holes show where rows of spikes would have been.

A world of seashells

Shells vary in size, shape and shade from place to place. Looking for them is enjoyable wherever in the world you are, but be sure only to pick up empty ones.

Family matters

Shells that belong to the same families generally live in similar conditions, even if they're in different parts of the world.

Wentletraps live in shallow water on any sandy shore.

Crenulated wentletrap

Precious wentletrap

Cool water shells

The cool seas surrounding northern Europe and North America are mostly home to small, tough shells.

European screw shells

Hallia

Mediterranean shells

The waters of the Mediterranean Sea between Europe and Africa are warm and calm. Many of its shells are small, or thin and delicate.

Rustic dove shell

Date mussel

Rosy tooth shell

Tropical shells

Tropical seas, around Australia, Africa and the Caribbean, contain the widest variety of large or colourful shells.

White banded bubble shells

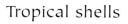

Distaff spindle

King helmet

Conch shells like this are found in the Bahamas. It's said you can hear the sea if you hold one to your ear.

Collecting and cleaning

Most of the fun of shell collecting is hunting for them, but you might want to take a few home too. Clean them thoroughly with warm, soapy water and a soft paintbrush, then leave them to dry on some paper.

Most empty bivalve shells are missing one half, though you might find a few with both.

It's wise not to buy exotic shells like these from shops. The animals they came from were probably killed illegally.

Seaside signals

Although the seashore is enjoyable to visit, it has many hazards too. Both the people on the shore and sailors at sea need signs to help keep them out of danger.

Safety on the shore

When the tide comes in, the water level can rise surprisingly fast. Flags or signs on the beach give warnings about whether conditions are safe.

Yellow and red flags mark out an area where lifeguards are on patrol.

*

*

A red flag means it's not safe to enter the sea.

Not all dangers carry warning signs. Help keep yourself safe by not going off exploring alone, and staying away from caves when the tide's coming in.

Lifebuoys like this can be thrown to swimmers in trouble.

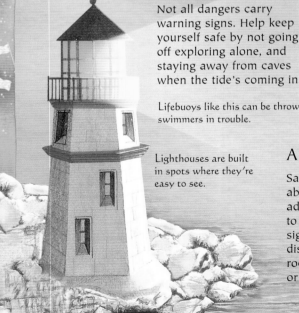

Lighthouses are built in spots where they're easy to see.

A guiding light

Sailors may need to know about a hazard far in advance, so they have time to react. Lighthouses flash signals to boats over long distances, warning them of rocks hidden under the water or guiding them through fog.

Message buoys

Buoys are floating plastic balls or platforms which give information. They can be used for anything from marking a safe route through the waters to monitoring weather, mooring boats or sending emergency signals.

A buoy with these markings warns that the area is dangerous.

This pattern on a buoy is used to indicate a safe area.

This buoy is supposed to mark a path for ships, but these sea lions are using it as a place to have a nap.

Flying the flag

Ships don't fly flags from their masts for decoration. Each one stands for both a letter of the alphabet and a message, which can be recognized by other sailors.

"A"

This flag is the letter "A". It's displayed when a diver's swimming under the boat.

*

"N"

"C"

"N" means "No" and "C" means "Yes". Flying them together is a distress signal.

Ocean bounty

Fish and other seafoods are well-known ocean resources. But the sea has many other treasures to offer, including fuels, medicines and gems.

Jewels of the ocean

The most precious jewels that come from the sea are pearls, which form inside a very small number of oysters. Other shells are used to make jewellery too, such as the shiny mother-of-pearl coating inside top shells and abalones.

Mother-of-pearl shimmers blue or grey in the light.

This oyster might be the only one in 10,000 that contains a pearl.

Feeding on weed

Seaweed is very versatile. It's a common ingredient in many oriental foods and, believe it or not, seaweed extract is also used to thicken ice cream and is even found in common household items such as toothpaste.

Dulse is an edible seaweed.

Useful waste

Seabird droppings, also known as guano, are one of the most effective forms of natural fertilizer – 30 times richer than farmyard manure. Guano is gathered from sea cliffs and exported around the world.

Layers of cormorant guano can be many metres thick.

Lifesavers

The healing power of plants has been recognized for many centuries, but the next generation of medicines might come from the ocean. These could include painkillers, surgical glue, cancer-fighting drugs and much more.

Some corals are so similar to human bone, they're used in operations.

Scientists think they might be able to make painkillers from deadly poison found in cone shells.

Certain types of sea slugs are being tested as a source of drugs to treat memory loss.

Fossil fuel

Over a fifth of the world's oil comes from the sea bed. Oil formed millions of years ago when the remains of sea creatures and plants sank to the bottom of the sea and broke down into an oozing black liquid, beneath layers of sand and rock.

When prehistoric sea animals and plants like these died, their bodies very slowly turned into oil.

Save Our Seas

For many centuries, people existed in harmony with the sea. In recent times, our changing lifestyles have started to make human beings an enemy to ocean life.

Oil spills

Lots of oil that people burn for fuel is transported in huge ships called tankers. If oil accidentally spills into the ocean, it forms a pool called a slick on the water's surface. Washed-up slicks pollute beaches and can kill wildlife.

*

Seabirds can't keep warm if their feathers are oily, so they die. Conservationists help the birds by scrubbing them clean.

Overfishing

Today's enormous fishing nets and use of electronic equipment to find fish lead to bigger catches than ever before. If fishermen catch too many of one type of fish, they risk causing it to die out. This is called overfishing.

Fishing with large nets can lead to other animals being caught along with the fish.

Many people are campaigning for fishing nets with larger holes, which allow young fish to escape and breed.

In 1977, fishing for herring was banned in the North Sea so their numbers could increase.

Beach invaders

Millions of holidaymakers visit beaches every year, with hotels constantly being built to accommodate them. The more of the coast that people take over, the less room there is for animals.

Beach tourism has driven Mediterranean monk seals to the verge of extinction.

This sea turtle comes ashore to breed. But humans on beaches scare turtles away.

What you can do

You might not be able to stop an oil slick, but you can help keep the shore clean by never leaving litter behind. At home, you could avoid eating species that are known to be overfished, or join an ocean conservation group. You can find out more on the Usborne Quicklinks Website at www.usborne-quicklinks.com.

Abandoned can-holders strangle animals. Help avoid this by cutting them up before you put them in the bin.

Myths and legends

The oceans have inspired storytellers throughout history, leading to dramatic tales of monsters, gods and ghosts. Could any of these legends be true?

King of the ocean

Many Ancient Greek myths feature gods and monsters of the deep. The ruler of them all was a god named Poseidon (known to the Romans as Neptune). He lived in an underwater palace made of coral and gems, and his anger was said to stir up violent storms.

Poseidon carried a magic trident that could create earthquakes.

Birth of a goddess

Venus, the Roman goddess of love and beauty, was born from ocean foam. She is traditionally shown standing on a giant clam shell with nature spirits called nymphs surrounding her. In Greek myths, Venus is called Aphrodite.

This picture shows the goddess Venus being born from the waves.

Animal gods

Supernatural sea dwellers are not only a feature of Greek myths. In Fiji, legend has it that the fierce shark god Dakuwanga ate fishermen, but was forced to change his ways by an octopus god who defeated him in battle.

The Fijian god Dakuwanga was said to take the form of a monstrous basking shark.

In stories, mermaids normally have long, flowing hair, which they spend hours combing.

Mermaids

Mermaids were fabled creatures with a woman's top half and a fish's tail. Stories exist all over the world of sailors who saw and fell in love with these seductive sea maidens.

Sand dollars are a type of urchin. Their empty shells are known as mermaids' money.

Moo maids

It's possible that sailors who thought they saw mermaids were actually seeing animals called sea cows. From a distance, they might look a little like humans with fish tails.

Up close, it's hard to imagine how anyone could mistake a sea cow for a mermaid.

Ghost ships

In the 17th and 18th centuries, reported sightings of ghostly ships were quite common. A ship called The Flying Dutchman was cursed to sail the world until the end of time, and even today it's rumoured to bring terrible bad luck to anyone who sees it.

German submariners claimed to see The Flying Dutchman during *World War II*.

A phantom ship called the Libera Nos is said to roam the oceans with a crew of skeletons.

Sea serpents

Throughout history, sailors have told tales of huge serpents swimming past their ships. Ocean-dwelling snakes really do exist but they're not very big, so the stories seem to be just that.

Most sea snakes are less than 1m (3ft) long.

Giant sea serpents like this almost certainly don't exist outside people's imaginations.

A land under the sea

The island of Atlantis was said to have been destroyed by an earthquake around 10,000BC, sinking into the sea without a trace. No one knows if it really existed or where it is, but guesses have included sites near Cuba, Gibraltar and even Antarctica.

Many stories mention the great wealth of Atlantis. Perhaps its treasures still lie beneath the waves.

Monsters of the deep

Stories of sea monsters are closely related to those of sea snakes. Perhaps the most horrifying of them all is the kraken which, according to legend, would wrap its immense tentacles around a ship to capsize it, then devour the crew.

Lake monsters, such as the mysterious Loch Ness Monster of Scotland, could be the last relatives of sea monsters – if they are real.

*

Real monsters?

Some of the people who claimed to see kraken and other vast sea creatures might have been describing giant squid. These creatures are known to live in the deep ocean, yet a live one has never been caught. An even larger "real monster", the colossal squid, is thought to live near the Antarctic.

No one has ever photographed a colossal squid. This computer image shows how experts think it might look.

251

Amazing but true

Largest fish
The largest recorded whale shark was 18m (59ft) long, and was estimated to weigh a whopping 48 tons.

Whale shark and diver

Clinging on
A limpet can cling to a rock so firmly that it would take a force 2,000 times its own weight to prise it off.

If a limpet is pulled off its rock, it might die.

Sweet sea holly
During the seventeenth and eighteenth centuries, sea holly roots were candied and eaten as a snack.

Pea crab in mussel shell

Tiniest crabs
Pea crabs are barely 6.5mm (a quarter of an inch) long. They live and feed inside oyster and mussel shells.

Ink-credible
Cuttlefish and squids squirt out a cloud of liquid called sepia to confuse their enemies. For many centuries, people used this to make ink.

Sepia is brown, like a cuttlefish's body.

*

Wonder whiskers
Walrus whiskers are so stiff, Inuit people use them as toothpicks.

Walrus

Bated breath
Sperm whales can hold their breath for up to two hours, the longest of any mammal.

Electric fish
The black torpedo ray can create electricity in its body – enough to power a TV in a short burst.

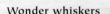

Awesome waves

The highest natural wave ever recorded was seen in the Pacific in 1933. It measured 34m (111.5ft), the height of a ten-storey building.

Deepest ocean bed

The deepest part of the Pacific Ocean is 11.033km (6.85 miles) deep. A 1kg steel ball would take just over an hour to sink to the bottom.

Sea salt

There's enough salt in the oceans to cover the land with a layer 150m (492ft) thick.

Tallest mountain

Earth's tallest mountain is Mauna Kea, which rises up 10,203m (33,474ft) from the floor of the Pacific Ocean.

Sea life

An estimated 80% of all living things on Earth exist beneath the ocean's surface.

Highest sea cliffs

The sea cliffs around Molokai, Hawaii, are as tall as three Eiffel Towers – that's over 960m (3,150ft).

Sunken gold

Sea water contains traces of many metals, including gold. If it could be extracted, there would be enough for everyone on Earth to have their own 4g (0.14oz) piece.

Coral reefs cover only 0.7% of the ocean floor, yet contain 25% of all known ocean species.

Colossal coral

Off the coast of north Australia lies the Great Barrier Reef – the longest coral reef on Earth. It's the biggest structure ever formed by a living thing and can even be seen from the Moon.

Ginormous jellyfish

Lion's mane jellyfish are the world's largest jellyfish. Their tentacles can grow over 30m (100ft) in length.

Lion's mane jellyfish

Salt surplus

As birds feed from the sea, they take in lots of salt water with their food. They get rid of the salt by letting it trickle out of their nostrils.

Acid attack

Tiger cowries can shoot out clouds of sulphuric acid to sting the eyes of a predator.

Water walkers

As a Wilson's storm petrel – one of the world's smallest sea birds – flutters above the sea, it pats the water with its feet. This makes it look like it's walking on water.

Wilson's storm petrel

Tremendous tides

The greatest tidal range in the world is in the Bay of Fundy, Canada. The water level can rise by as much as 15m (50ft) during each tide.

Roaming eye

A baby flatfish hatches with an eye on either side of its head. Over the next few weeks, one eye moves around so that both eyes end up on the same side.

Flatfish

Heavyweight shell

Giant clams have the largest shells. They can grow up to 1.2m (4ft) wide and can weigh over a quarter of a tonne.

Giant clam

Super seaweed

Pacific giant kelp is not only the longest seaweed but also the fastest growing plant in the world. It grows to around 60m (200ft) long, at a rate of 0.5m (1 ½ ft) a day.

Stinging snacks

Some types of sea slug can eat a jellyfish's stinging cells without harming themselves. The cells pass through the slug's body and move to its tentacles so it can use them for its own defence.

Giant kelp

Difficult birth

Mediterranean multi-armed starfish can reproduce by tearing themselves in two. It takes several months for the two "children" to grow into complete starfish.

Mediterranean multi-armed starfish

Puffing up

When attacked, puffer fish gulp water and swell up like a balloon. Many have spiky scales which stand up like needles when the fish inflates.

Pufferfish can puff up to three times their normal size.

Blue-ringed octopus

Small but deadly

It may only be the size of a golfball, but a blue-ringed octopus is one of the most poisonous sea creatures. Each one contains enough venom to kill 25 men, and there is no known antidote to the poison.

Lobster conga

Each year in the USA, thousands of spiny lobsters migrate along Florida's Atlantic coast. They march in single file in groups of about 50, each with its claws hooked round the lobster in front.

Garden Wildlife

Garden wildlife

To many people, a garden is just a place to relax and have fun. But to animals, it's a breeding ground, food store and hideaway rolled into one.

Living together

All animals rely on plants, or other animals, for food. The many creatures that feed together in a garden show how things in nature are linked.

Butterflies and bees feed from flowers.

Ladybirds eat tiny bugs that live on plants.

Bringing up babies

Most animals need a place to find a mate and have babies. A garden's varied landscape is ideal for this, giving them protection and often a source of food for their family, too.

Gardens supply birds with a place to nest, and worms to feed their chicks.

Ideal homes

A place that has all the things an animal needs to survive is called a habitat. A garden is full of different habitats, each one with just the right conditions for something to live there.

Look in soil and under rocks for scuttling animals such as woodlice.

Some insects build their nests in holes in walls.

Wall mason wasp

Garden snail

Centipede

Rotting compost is home to worms, beetles and centipedes.

Flowerbeds offer shelter to snails, slugs and caterpillars.

Woodlouse

A helping hand

Although it's enjoyable simply to go outside and see what animals are around, there are many easy things you can do to make gardens even more enticing for them. Throughout this book, you'll find ideas for ways to turn an ordinary garden into a thriving wildlife garden.

This tiny mammal is a shrew. Shrews can be attracted to gardens just by letting a patch of wild grasses grow in a quiet corner.

A bird garden

No matter what the season, birds will always visit gardens. You can attract more by providing plenty of places for them to eat, bathe and nest.

Trees and hedges

Leafy branches are not only nesting sites for birds, but also well-stocked larders. Their fruits are an important source of food, especially in autumn, when insects die away.

Berries from Highclere holly bushes keep hungry birds, such as this redwing, fed in the harsh winter months.

The berries that grow on rowan trees keep birds fed in late autumn.

Birds feed on hawthorns' autumn berries, and nest and roost in their dense branches.

Thick bramble bushes provide shelter for birds and bear blackberries for them to eat in autumn.

Chaffinch nesting in ivy

Climbing plants

Small birds find shelter in dense climbing plants, such as clematis, ivy and honeysuckle. Honeysuckle is also a source of pollen and nectar, and ivy provides berries in winter.

Honeysuckle

Flowery feeders

Finches and sparrows gobble up seeds that
they pluck directly from plants. If you grow
some of the plants shown here, you might
find different types of birds perching on them
in the summer, pecking away at their seeds.

House sparrows crack
sunflower seed shells
with their stout beaks.

Both the seeds and leaves
of dandelion plants are a
treat for greenfinches.

Goldfinches feast
on a thistle's
downy seeds.

Creepy crawly corner

If you leave a corner of a garden to grow wild,
you'll soon find plants, such as buttercups, daisies
and thistles, springing up. These flowers and
grasses attract insects which, in turn, encourage
visits from insect-eating birds. You could also dig
over a patch of soil in a garden, making it easier
for birds to find worms and other creepy crawlies.

Birds are
attracted to
the insects
that feed
on these
plants.

Shepherd's
purse

Creeping
buttercup

Daisy

Soft brome

Bird boxes

As winter ends, birds start looking for a place to nest. Many garden birds use bird boxes, as the spread of towns and farms has taken over a lot of their natural nesting sites. Put up a bird box or two to see if any birds move in. You can buy different kinds that best suit particular birds.

For house martins, a rounded type of bird box that can be fixed under the edge of a roof is best.

Closed boxes with small entrance holes are good for little birds, such as tits.

A tree trunk or an ivy-covered wall is an ideal spot to hang a bird box.

The right place

Bird boxes need to be hung as high as possible, in a quiet area. Don't hang them anywhere that gets lots of direct sunlight, such as a wall that faces south, because too much heat is bad for baby birds.

If a box is too small inside, a bird may lay fewer eggs. The floor area should be at least 130cm² (20in²).

Building supplies

You can encourage birds to build a nest in your garden by leaving out nesting materials for them. From fences and trees, you can hang feathers, pet fur, bits of wool or even hair from a comb or brush.

This great tit has lined its nest with hair and fluffy feathers.

Look for feathers in the places where you've seen birds feeding.

Water for all

Water is just as vital for birds as food and shelter. To make sure they have a supply all year round, you could put out a bird bath or deep plant pot saucer, and fill it with water. In winter, the water might freeze, so remember to break the ice if this happens.

Birds enjoy fresh water, so clean out your bird bath regularly.

Safety measures

Birds can become entangled in loose netting, so if there's any in the garden – stretched across a pond or a vegetable patch – make sure it's pulled tight. Also, it's best to wait until late summer to trim hedges, to avoid hurting any chicks that might be tucked away in nests inside.

Nesting season signs

The breeding and nesting season is a busy time for birds. With so much going on, it's not hard to see signs of birds raising a family.

First things first

Before they even start the difficult task of raising their young, birds must first find a mate and build a nest.

Look out and listen for a bird singing in the same place every day. This robin could be attracting a mate, or defending its home.

Many male birds, like the starlings shown here, fight over who owns a nesting area.

*

*
In the spring, you'll often see birds carrying nesting materials. Magpies use large twigs.

Building a nest

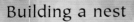

Nests come in many shapes and sizes, because each type of bird uses different materials and techniques to build them.

House martins gather mud and use it to build mud cups, which they stick onto ledges and walls.

Keeping warm

Birds use their bodies to keep their eggs warm enough to hatch. Some pluck off a clump of feathers, leaving an area of warm skin – a brood patch – to press against the eggs.

This marsh tit will warm its eggs with its bare skin.

Finding food

When the eggs have hatched, the parents must work hard to feed their ever-hungry babies. They might fly to and from the nest several hundred times a day with titbits to eat.

Baby thrushes open their mouths wide to beg for food.

Cleaning up

As well as delivering food to the nest, you might spot parent birds carrying droppings away from the nest, trying to keep the area clean for their chicks.

This stonechat has its chicks' droppings in its beak.

Creepy crawlies

Even the smallest garden contains hundreds of creepy crawlies. There are many different types to look out for, each with its own unique features.

Insects

Most of the tiny creatures you'll see in a garden are insects. Every insect has six legs, a pair of antennae, and usually one or two pairs of wings (though these might be hard to see).

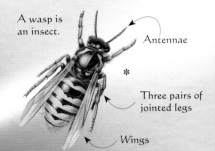

A wasp is an insect.

Antennae

*

Three pairs of jointed legs

Wings

Eight-legged creatures

Spiders, harvestmen and mites all belong to a group of creepy crawlies with eight legs. They usually feed on smaller animals, and a few are poisonous.

This close-up picture of a spider shows tiny hairs on its body, which it uses to sense the world around it.

Most kinds of mites are very tiny. Red spider mites like these are easiest to spot on walls or paving slabs.

Lots of legs

Millipedes and centipedes are types of creepy crawlies with many legs. You'll find them in dark, damp places, such as under bark and in soil, but they don't like light, so they often scurry away when exposed.

Centipedes are hunters. They stab their prey with poisoned claws.

Some snake millipedes have up to 700 legs.

Although "centipede" means "100 legs", they have between 30 and 70.

Long antennae for touching and smelling

Woodlice

Peek under a large stone and you're sure to see woodlice. These belong to a group of animals with hard body armour and more than six legs. They are more closely related to crabs than insects.

A woodlouse's body armour is made of overlapping sections.

Woodlice grow by shedding their hard coverings.

Pill bugs are a type of woodlouse that can roll into a tight ball.

Which is which?

It can be hard to tell some types of creepy crawlies apart. If you spot a tiny creature, notice its markings, the number of legs, whether it has wings, and how it behaves. A field guide will help you to identify it.

Water boatmen are insects, but some of their six legs are hard to see.

Its eight legs tell you that this harvestman is related to spiders.

Insect world

Insects are intriguing and complex creatures. They often look and behave differently at each stage of their lives, so watch out for both adults and babies in gardens.

Laying eggs

Almost all insects make babies by pairing up with a mate. After this, the female lays eggs. She usually chooses a safe spot on or near something that the young insects can eat when they hatch.

Lacewing eggs have stalks attached, to keep hungry ants from reaching them.

A potter wasp's young hatch from eggs in clay "pots". They are fed on caterpillars.

Growth and change

Many insects start off as babies called larvae. For most of their lives larvae look nothing like their parents, but when they reach a certain age they transform inside cocoons called pupae. You might see these on trees, fences and walls.

Meadow brown butterfly

1. Like most insects, adult butterflies lay eggs.

*

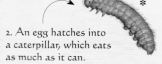

2. An egg hatches into a caterpillar, which eats as much as it can. *

3. The caterpillar's skin hardens and becomes a pupa. *

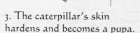

4. Inside the pupa, the caterpillar's body changes. It emerges as a butterfly. *

Mini adults

Insects such as dragonflies hatch from their eggs already looking like miniature adults. At this stage the young are called nymphs. A nymph grows by shedding its skin from time to time until it reaches full size. Look for dragonflies and old skins if there's a pond nearby.

Female

Male

1. These dragonflies are mating. Next, the female will lay her eggs.

2. Each egg hatches into a nymph. It spends two years growing and shedding its skin.

Old skin

This dragonfly nymph has climbed out of its skin to become an adult.

Insect parents

Insects usually look after their eggs until they hatch. Some even take care of their young after that, too. Others, such as moths and butterflies, abandon the eggs after they are laid.

If you get too near an earwig's eggs, their mother will snap her pincers at you.

Hidden babies

Some young insects are harder to spot than others. Froghopper nymphs, for instance, are hidden inside blobs of foam on plant stems.

Adult froghopper

Close-up of young froghopper

The foam is sometimes called cuckoo spit.

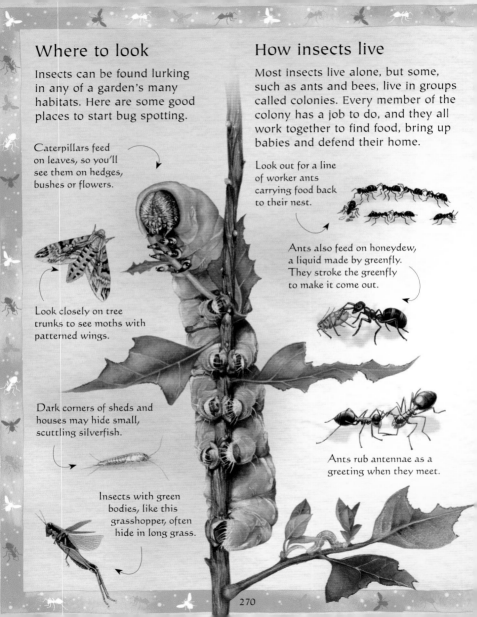

Where to look

Insects can be found lurking in any of a garden's many habitats. Here are some good places to start bug spotting.

Caterpillars feed on leaves, so you'll see them on hedges, bushes or flowers.

Look closely on tree trunks to see moths with patterned wings.

Dark corners of sheds and houses may hide small, scuttling silverfish.

Insects with green bodies, like this grasshopper, often hide in long grass.

How insects live

Most insects live alone, but some, such as ants and bees, live in groups called colonies. Every member of the colony has a job to do, and they all work together to find food, bring up babies and defend their home.

Look out for a line of worker ants carrying food back to their nest.

Ants also feed on honeydew, a liquid made by greenfly. They stroke the greenfly to make it come out.

Ants rub antennae as a greeting when they meet.

A garden buffet

Almost everything in a garden is food for one insect or another. This includes leaves, plant roots, rubbish, animals' blood, dung and even other insects.

Wasps eat sweet things like this spilled marmalade.

Robber flies act like vampires, pouncing on their victims and sucking out their juices.

Self-defence

All insects face the threat of big, hungry enemies, but many have clever ways of hiding or protecting themselves. See how many you can spot.

*

Enemies think this hoverfly is a wasp, but it's really a harmless lookalike.

*

This comma butterfly is well disguised among dead leaves.

Hungry animals mistake the shapes on an eyed hawkmoth's wings for a scary enemy's eyes.

*

Useful insects

As well as being food for many other creatures, insects are important for other reasons too. Some of the vital things they do include burying the bodies of dead animals and helping plants to make seeds.

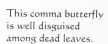

Burying beetles bury dead animals by digging earth from beneath them. They feed on the bodies.

Pollen carriers

Most garden flowers produce a powder called pollen, which is carried around by insects. Without this help, flowers couldn't make seeds to grow into new plants.

A sweet treat

Insects visit flowers to drink a sweet liquid called nectar. As they seek their prize, pollen sticks to their bodies. The insects carry it to other flowers of the same kind, which can then make fruits with seeds inside.

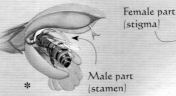

Female part (stigma)

Male part (stamen)

Pollen rubs off a flower's male part onto the bee's body as it drinks nectar.

When the insect visits another flower, the pollen sticks to its female part.

Busy bees

A bee spends its whole day buzzing from flower to flower, drinking nectar and gathering pollen. If you watch a bee on its trips, you'll see it only visits one sort of flower at a time.

This honey bee is picking up pollen grains as it clambers over flowers.

Moths

You can identify a moth by its feathery antennae.

Moths mostly drink nectar at night. Their sensitive antennae can detect a flower's delicious scent in the dark.

Butterflies

Butterflies feed on nothing but nectar during their short adult lives. Most of them only survive long enough to mate and lay eggs, sometimes less than a week.

This swallowtail butterfly is drinking nectar from a lavender flower.

Drinking tubes

Most pollen carriers have a mouthpart called a proboscis, which sucks up nectar like a drinking straw. Butterflies and moths unfurl their long mouthparts to reach into flowers.

A butterfly's proboscis curls up when it's not being used.

Other pollen carriers

A few types of flies, beetles and wasps also feed on nectar. Most of them have fairly short mouthparts, so they tend to feed on flat, open flowers where the nectar is easy to reach.

Look out for wasps, beetles and flies on flowers with a flattish shape.

Wasp on Michaelmas daisy

Dronefly on hogweed

Web weavers

Spiders look a bit like insects, but they are actually creatures called arachnids. Spiders are helpful garden visitors, because they eat bugs that harm plants.

Wonderful webs

The most well-known feature of spiders is their ability to spin delicate, silky webs. These act as traps to catch the insects they feed on. Webs are easiest to see when they're wet, so look for them after rain, or early on a dewy morning.

A garden spider can spin an intricate orb web like this one in about an hour.

House spiders spin sheet webs (also called cobwebs) in corners.

Wall spiders spin tube-like webs in cracks in walls. Bugs fall inside.

Webless spiders

Not all spiders spin webs to catch food. Some attack their prey directly by pouncing and grabbing.

Crab spiders can run sideways like a crab. They seize insects with their front legs.

Caught in a trap

You won't always see spiders on their webs – they usually hide nearby. When an insect becomes snagged, the spider rushes out to stab it with its deadly fangs.

Sometimes, you might see a spider binding an insect in threads before eating it.

A dangerous date

Female garden spiders are bigger than males, and more vicious. When a male approaches a female to mate, he spins an escape thread so he can get away quickly if she attacks. He may have to approach her many times before she allows him to mate.

Escape thread

Male garden spider

Female garden spider

Mother spiders

Female spiders are good parents. Some mother spiders hide their eggs to keep them safe, but others wrap them up and take them wherever they go.

This wolf spider is carrying her eggs in a ball of protective web threads.

*

Slugs and snails

Unlike other kinds of creepy crawlies, slugs and snails have no legs at all. They creep around slowly on a slick of slime, looking for plants to nibble.

Spot the difference

Snails and slugs are alike in many ways, but it's easy to tell them apart. Snails have hard shells on their backs, and almost all slugs don't.

Snails and slugs have one pair of tentacles for seeing and a smaller pair for touching.

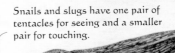

Grey slug

Snails and slugs leave behind a silvery trail of slime wherever they go.

The snail trail

During the day, snails and slugs cluster together in damp, sheltered spots. At night or after rain, they go out to feed, usually returning afterwards to where they started. Find these meeting places by following the shiny trails the slimy creatures left behind.

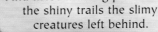

You can see the slime glistening on this snail's body.

Rasping tongues

Snails and slugs eat both fresh and rotting leaves, sometimes doing a lot of damage to garden plants. They feed using rows of tiny saw-like teeth on their tongue. Listen to one closely and you might be able to hear its tongue rasping.

Look for holes left behind in plants after slugs have finished eating.

Safety first

A snail can retreat into its shell when threatened, or if the weather is too cold or dry. Slugs burrow into the soil to keep their bodies moist, or repel enemies by curling up and making thick, nasty-tasting goo.

Black slug

Slugs squish their bodies into a ball if something tries to harm them.

Snails can seal up their shell with a plug of dried mucus.

Male and female

In spring and summer, you might see a pair of snails coming together to make eggs. They crawl over each other for several hours before starting to mate.

Brown-lipped snails preparing to mate

*

Usually, female animals lay eggs, but a snail is both male and female. After mating, both partners lay many eggs in the soil. These hatch into tiny snails a few weeks later.

Snail eggs look like pale balls.

*

Water babies

Even a tiny garden pond is home to many animals, including bugs, snails, and amphibians such as frogs. Amphibians have their babies in water, so ponds are vital to their survival.

Fascinating frogs

Like all amphibians, frogs are born in water but spend time on land, too. During winter, many avoid the cold by sleeping in mud on the pond bottom. In spring, the water comes alive with frisky frogs looking for a partner.

Frogs catch bugs with their sticky tongues.

Long back legs for jumping

This frog is puffing up its throat to croak. The sound attracts a mate.

Warts and all

Toads are very similar to frogs, but with dumpier bodies and dry, warty skin. You're not likely to see a toad during the day, as they tend to hide in burrows and under rocks.

A toad has shorter back legs than a frog.

People used to think that touching a toad gave you warts.

Newts

Newts are a type of amphibian with a long tail and smooth skin. The best time to see them in garden ponds is between April and June, when they breed.

Female smooth newts have dull brown bodies.

Males have patterned bodies and crests on their tails.

Having babies

Amphibians' eggs are called spawn. Frogspawn comes in big, wobbly clumps, whereas toadspawn is laid in long strings. Look for spawn in shallow areas of a pond. Each egg hatches into a baby called a tadpole, which looks very different from its parents.

Newts lay their eggs individually on pond plants.

A young newt has tiny legs, and feathery gills for breathing.

These pictures show how much a tadpole changes as it grows into a frog.

Tadpole at 1 week old

8 weeks old

11 weeks old

Adult frog

A ribbon of toadspawn can be up to 2m (6.5ft) long.

This frog is surrounded by its spawn. The black blobs will become tadpoles.

A wildlife pond

Natural ponds and pools are becoming more rare, but a garden pond offers animals water to drink or live in instead.

Making a pond

If you want to create a simple wildlife pond, you'll need pond liner, rocks and a square metre or so of space.

Dig your pond in a sunny spot away from trees, so fallen leaves won't make the water dirty.

Spring is the best time of year for pond-making.

Dig the shelf about 15cm (6in) down.

1. Dig a hole about 60cm (24in) deep, 70cm (28in) wide and 1m (40in) long, with gently sloping sides.

2. Dig a shallow shelf all around the side of the hole, so animals can climb in and out.

3. Completely cover the sides and bottom of the hole with sheets of newspaper.

You can buy pond liner at a garden centre.

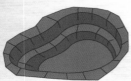

Cover the exposed liner between the rocks with soil.

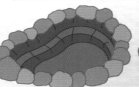

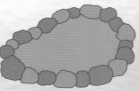

4. Line the pond with liner, leaving about 20cm (8in) extra all around the edge.

5. Use stones to weigh down the extra liner all around the hole.

6. Fill the pond with tapwater from a hose, or rainwater from a water butt.

Choosing plants

The most important things to put in a new pond are plants – a mix of floating types to create shade for creatures under the water, and waterweeds to give them oxygen. Some plants spread very fast, so you might need to remove a few now and again.

Shallow-water flowers can stand on the pond's shelf in pots, or you can pin their roots down with stones.

Bur-reed

Water soldier

Stones

These plants attach themselves to the pond bottom by long stems.

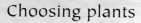

Broad-leaved pondweed

Water crowfoot

The leaves of these plants float on the water's surface.

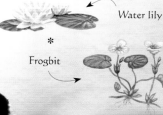

Water lily

*

Frogbit

Algae are microscopic plants which appear by themselves in all ponds.

Pond animals

There's no need to buy any animals to put in a pond. Simply add the plants and wait for the local wildlife to move in.

All kinds of animals will want to visit a new pond, including thirsty birds like this goldfinch.

Fish

Some people like to put fish in their garden ponds. It's better not to, though, as they eat tadpoles and frogspawn, as well as the bugs and plants that wild garden visitors feed on.

A big pond might attract herons, which eat both fish and frogs.

Pond insects

Ponds are home to hundreds of insects. Some, such as dragonflies, start their lives in the water, then leave when they're fully grown and return as adults to lay eggs. Others spend their whole lives there.

*

This spectacular emperor dragonfly is shown life-sized.

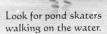

Look for pond skaters walking on the water.

Other pond life

Some animals that you can see on land, such as spiders and snails, have relatives that live in ponds. Look for them on pond plants, both above and below the water's surface.

Water spiders live under water. They make a "tent" from a bubble of air.

Tiny creatures

Ponds are teeming with animals that are almost too small to see. Larger animals feed on them.

In real life, these water fleas are barely bigger than a pinhead.

Ramshorn snails lay their eggs on pond plants.

A mini marsh

Many pond creatures also thrive in marshy areas. To make one, dig a hole about 10cm (4in) deep and 40cm (16in) wide and line it with pond liner. Fill it with water, then add some soil to create a shallow mudpool.

These flowers will grow well in a marsh.

Yellow flag

Grass snakes might visit your marsh. Don't worry, they're harmless to people.

Marsh marigold

Purple loosestrife

Stone shelters

Toads and frogs need dark places to hide when they're not in the water. The best sort of shelter is a rockery made of large, flattish stones or bricks, piled up loosely so the animals can wriggle beneath. Lizards and snakes might rest there, too.

Slow worms like to hide under rocks. They're actually a type of lizard.

The stones on the right are surrounded by heather. Planting rockery flowers attracts bugs for larger animals to eat.

Purple aubretia

Starry saxifrage

Under the ground

Even the parts of a garden you can't see are full of life.
Animals make their homes and search for food under
the ground, just as they do in the world above.

Underground nurseries

Many insects lay their eggs in soil.
When the larvae hatch out, they
feed on plant roots. Several
years might pass before
you see them on the
surface as adults.

A cranefly's
larva is called
a leatherjacket.

Cranefly

Moth caterpillars
grow in cocoons.

Dot
moth

Cockchafer
beetle

Beetle larvae
are also known
as grubs.

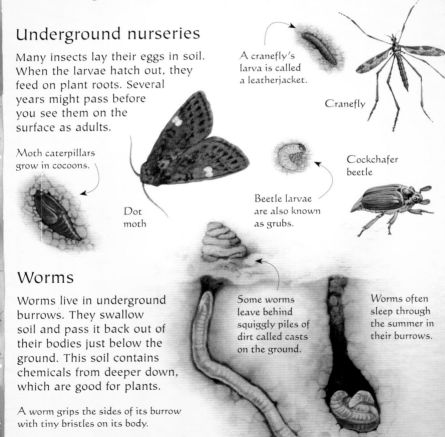

Worms

Worms live in underground
burrows. They swallow
soil and pass it back out of
their bodies just below the
ground. This soil contains
chemicals from deeper down,
which are good for plants.

A worm grips the sides of its burrow
with tiny bristles on its body.

Some worms
leave behind
squiggly piles of
dirt called casts
on the ground.

Worms often
sleep through
the summer in
their burrows.

Worm watching

Worms are important garden animals because they keep the soil rich by churning it up. You can make this simple wormery to see how.

You will need:
- a large jar ✸ fine sand
- soil ✸ paper ✸ string
- a cluster of leaves
- some earthworms

Tie the paper in place with the string.

Return the worms to the garden afterwards.

1. Put alternating layers of sand and soil in the jar. Place the leaves on top, as food for the worms.

2. Dig up some worms and put them in the jar. Wrap paper around it to keep out light.

3. After two days, remove the paper. See how the worms have mixed up the layers.

Digging machines

Moles spend most of their time digging tunnels and hunting for worms. When they come to the surface it's usually to find a mate, or to hunt for food on a damp night. Telltale mounds of earth called molehills show where they've been.

Moles have long, sharp claws for digging, and sensitive noses for sniffing out food.

Night-time

When you go to sleep, some animals are only just waking up. Most come out at dusk, but others emerge later and stay up until dawn.

The night shift

You'd be surprised at the number and variety of creatures that lurk in your garden in the dark. If you go out with a torch, here are some of the things you might see. Be as quiet as you can.

Green lacewings rest on trees and bushes.

Beetles fly around, attracted to lights.

Male dark bush crickets chirp loudly on summer evenings.

Wood mice come out in the dark to climb bushes and feed on their berries.

Female glow-worms light up their bodies to attract males. They are very rare garden visitors.

This tawny owl is swooping down to catch a mouse in its razor-sharp claws.

Owls

Owls are meat eaters. They hunt for mice and other small animals, and may even attack other birds. Owls fly almost silently, but you might hear them make a "hoo hoo" call while they are resting in trees.

Bats

Bats can often be seen at dusk, swooping over gardens to catch flying bugs. They sleep through winter, so you're most likely to see them in the warmer months.

The pipistrelle is the most common garden bat. Its body is small enough to fit in a matchbox.

Late bloomers

If you plant a mixture of night-blooming flowers like the ones shown here, they will attract lots of different moths. These, in turn, will attract hungry bats.

Honeysuckle and evening primrose are night-blooming flowers that are often visited by moths.

Furry creatures

Badgers, mice and other furry creatures come to gardens to feed. You're less likely to see them than birds or bugs, though, as they are shy around people.

Badgers

Badgers sometimes visit gardens in the countryside. They snuffle around looking for earthworms, often digging up flowerbeds as they go.

*

You can recognize a badger by its stripy face.

Foxes

Foxes used to be only countryside animals, but the loss of their natural habitat has led them to towns and cities too. You might see one running across a road, or sniffing around bins at twilight for scraps to eat.

This type of fox, called a red fox, is the only one you're likely to see in a garden.

Mice and rats

Mice and rats eat almost anything, and will move into your house if they get the chance. It's best not to drive them away completely, because they're eaten by owls, but don't encourage them. Keep the ground clear of food scraps from bins and bird feeders.

As their name suggests, woodmice usually live in woods, but can visit gardens too.

Brown rats often hide under sheds, coming out at dusk to feed.

House mice sometimes nest in secret corners of houses and sheds.

Shrews

Shrews are mouse-sized animals with tiny, sharp teeth for biting into creepy crawlies. A shrew must eat its own body weight in food every day to survive.

Shrews come out at night to hunt for slugs and worms. In the daytime they hide under plants.

Dormice

Dormice look a bit like little fat squirrels. These rare creatures nest in trees or sometimes in the roofs of buildings. Some types can occasionally be seen hanging acrobatically from bird feeders, nibbling away at peanuts.

Edible dormouse

Polecats

Polecats live in areas where there is plenty of cover, such as low trees and hedges. They sometimes use holes under a garden shed or decking as a place to build a den and raise their young.

This polecat is hunting, sniffing the air for insects, birds or small mammals.

Weasels

Weasels tend to be shy, usually staying in long grass or thick hedges. They can come to gardens to look for prey, such as rodents, birds and rabbits.

Weasels

Stoats

Stoat

Stoats are good climbers and you might spot one clambering up creeping plants, to raid birds' nests in trees and under the roofs of houses. In northern areas during winter, stoats develop a white winter coat, called ermine.

A stoat's pure white winter coat provides good camouflage against its snowy northern habitat.

Roe deer

Roe deer have red coats in the summer, which turn grey in winter. You can recognize a male by the spiky antlers on its head. Deer very occasionally come to gardens to eat flowers and shrubs.

Heather plants are one of a roe deer's favourite snacks.

Rabbits

Rabbits are often seen as pests by gardeners because they uproot new plants, strip bark from trees, and dig holes in lawns. Dawn and dusk are best times times of day to spot a rabbit.

Rabbits live in groups of two or three males, three or four females, and their young.

Don't feed the animals

Although it's tempting to attract furry creatures, such as foxes and badgers, by leaving out food, it's better not to. Feeding these animals makes them too dependent on people, so the best way to help them is to leave them to scavenge or hunt for themselves.

Foxes are excellent hunters. They kill small animals by rearing up and stamping on them.

Mouse

A winter rest

Winter is the toughest season for wildlife. Food is scarce, and temperatures are low. At this time of year, animals need your help the most.

A big sleep

Sleeping through the winter is called hibernation. Most hibernating animals hide away in a shelter, such as a burrow or a hollow log. If you find a hibernating animal, leave it in peace.

Pipistrelle bats huddle up in old trees, or even in people's attics.

Hedgehogs curl up and sleep in leaf piles.

The hunt for food

Hibernating animals eat lots before they sleep, to avoid starving during winter. Many other animals face a struggle to find food in the cold.

A well-stocked feeder could be a hungry bird's ticket to survival.

Snack storage

Some animals survive winter by planning ahead. Squirrels, for instance, hide nuts in autumn to dig up and eat in winter.

A squirrel can sniff out buried nuts when it needs a meal.

Sun seekers

Another way that animals can deal with the cold is to go to a warmer country. When the seasons change again, they travel all the way back to where they started.

Swift

Swallow

Watch for these birds arriving in the summer.

Winter bugs

Many bugs spend winter sleeping in pupae or plant stems. But some, such as spiders, aren't affected by the cold. You'll see them going about their business as normal.

Bark beetles hibernate in tree bark, or under dead leaves.

A spider's body contains chemicals that act as natural antifreeze.

Most butterflies and moths spend winter safe inside a pupa.

A bug hotel

You can offer hibernating insects a safe place to stay by making this simple bug hotel.

You will need:
❋ a bunch of hollow garden canes or drinking straws ❋ string

Canes or straws of varying widths will attract different bugs.

1. Tie the straws or canes together in the middle with string.

2. Tie some more string, about 50cm (20in) long, around the middle.

3. Attach the bug hotel to a tree branch and wait for your guests to arrive.

Wildlife detectives

Garden visitors can be hard to spot. You'll never see every single creature that comes to a garden, but you might be able to find proof that they were there.

Plant clues

Leaves often reveal a lot about a visitor's activities. Leaf-cutter bees, for instance, tear up rose leaves to make nests for their eggs. Some insect larvae eat leaves from the inside, leaving trail-like marks as they go.

When this leaf-cutter bee has finished, it will leave behind a crescent-shaped hole.

The blotches on these leaves, called leaf mines, are tunnels left by hungry larvae.

Flowers, fungi and fruit

In spring, try looking at young plants to see if their flowers or leaves have been pecked by hungry birds. Autumn is a good time to look out for mushrooms, toadstools and fallen fruit that have been pecked, chewed, nibbled or gnawed by birds or rodents.

Pecked by sparrow

Pecked by blackbird

Gnawed by wood mouse

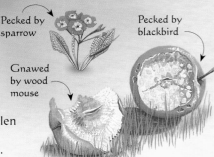

Tree signs

Nibbled pine cones and nuts are a sure sign that something has had a meal in a garden. Look out for empty nut shells on the ground beneath trees, or even stored in cracks in the bark. Cones are more common if there are pine trees nearby. Most animal species tackle their food differently, so check for teeth or beak marks.

Squirrels remove the scales completely from a pine cone, leaving a rough-looking stem.

A woodpecker shreds the scales to get to the seeds inside.

Spotted woodpeckers sometimes wedge cones in tree bark to shred them.

A squirrel has split this hazelnut shell at the top, and gnawed it near the base.

A blue tit chipped away this walnut's shell to reach the tasty treat inside.

A hawfinch cracked this cherry stone in half. Many seed-eating birds do this.

Bark damage

You can look in tree trunks for signs of insects and mammals. Deer and squirrels tear strips off trunks, and tiny bark beetles bore tunnels into bark.

Strip

Tunnels

3mm

Elm bark beetle

Footprints

Animals can leave distinctive tracks in soft mud or snow. Finding a trail of footprints can not only give you clues to the type of animal that made it, but also where it was going and how it was moving.

Fore (front) foot	Hind (back) foot
	*

Fore foot	Hind foot
	*

Fore foot	Hind foot
	*

A fox makes neat, dog-like prints in a straight line.

A badger's wide prints show five toes with sharp claws.

Cat prints show no claw marks.

The blackbird tracks below are paired, so you can tell that the bird was hopping along.

A single line of fox tracks shows that the fox was trotting, placing its back feet in the prints made by its front feet.

Direction of travel

Telltale droppings

If you find animal droppings, their shape and colour, location or even what they contain, could help you identify what left them. A mammal might leave its droppings in the place where it has been feeding; look for a bird's droppings under trees. But remember never to touch droppings you find.

Hedgehog droppings are black, and often contain shiny insect remains.

Badgers leave their droppings in specially dug holes.

White liquid droppings are left by starlings.

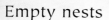

Empty nests

In the autumn, birds leave their nests empty after their chicks have flown away. Try looking for nests in trees or hedges, or on walls. It's important never to touch a nest, though – even ones that look abandoned could be used again the next year.

Song thrushes build bowl-like nests in hedges.

Rooks nest high up in trees and rooftops, usually in colonies.

Long-tailed tits make egg-shaped nests in brambles or gorse.

Home sweet home

It's not just birds who make their homes in gardens. Other animals, such as squirrels and dormice also build nests in undergrowth, trees and bushes, while moles and rats burrow into the ground.

Rats can burrow under sheds, and into soil and compost heaps.

In summer, dormice have been known to nest in bird nesting boxes.

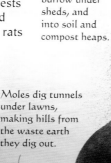

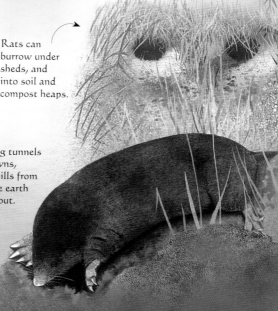

Moles dig tunnels under lawns, making hills from the waste earth they dig out.

Surprising visitors

Sometimes, you might see unexpected animals in a garden. Most come from nearby habitats, but others could be stopping to take a rest on a long journey.

Local wildlife

The types of animals found in a garden depend on where it is. So if you live near, say, a moor, you'll see different garden visitors from someone living near the coast.

Near woodland

A wood full of mature trees makes a perfect habitat for many kinds of animals. Rare bats, birds, butterflies and deer might pay gardens a visit if there is woodland nearby.

Long-eared bat

*

Roe deer are timid, but they occasionally venture into gardens near to woodlands.

Speckled wood butterfly

Near heathland

Reptiles are normally hard to find in gardens, but if you're near a heath you stand a much better chance of seeing one.

Common adders are poisonous. They rarely hurt people, though.

Near water

Water always attracts living things, so in a garden near the sea, a river or a marsh you'll see an even wider selection of animals and plants.

Yellow wagtails live near to rivers inland, and by salt marshes near the sea.

Sand wasps live in nests on beaches.

Burnet rose is a common wild flower around the coast.

Near fields

Fields are home to many small mammals, which will sometimes visit gardens to search for food.

Weasels hunt for birds, insects and other mammals.

Rabbits

Passing through

Some types of birds make trips to other countries each year, to find food and raise a family. If they stop to rest, or get blown off course, they could end up in a garden.

Whinchats spend winter in Africa, but they're very occasionally seen in British gardens during summer.

In the treetops

Trees are the largest flowering plants on Earth. They offer many things to wildlife: safe spots to make a home, shade from the sun, and plenty of things to eat.

Branches

Birds often nest in the branches of trees, or use them as perches. Squirrels also build their leafy nests where the branches join the trunk.

Grey squirrels like this one are expert climbers and acrobats, using their tails to balance and their claws to grip.

Leaves

Leaves are very important to a tree, as they make food that keeps it alive. They also act as handy places for insects to rest or lay their eggs.

The swellings on this leaf are called galls. They're made by various bugs laying eggs inside it.

*

Cherry galls

Spangle galls

Kidney galls

Bug-filled bark

A tree's trunk is covered in hard bark. As some types of bark get older they develop cracks, where creepy crawlies set up home.

A treecreeper probes cracks in tree bark to find bugs to eat.

Springtime blossom

In spring, trees burst into flower. Some types of blossom contain sweet nectar, which insects drink. Look for bees and wasps flying from tree to tree to sip nectar.

Apple blossom's aroma attracts bees and other pollen carriers.

Fruits and seeds

After pollen carriers have visited a tree flower, it develops into a fruit with seeds inside. Fruits are eaten by birds, which carry away the seeds in their bodies or drop them on the ground.

Cherries are eaten by bugs and birds in summer.

Jays eat acorns, the fruit of oak trees.

Blackthorn berries, called sloes, grow in the autumn.

Holly berries are an important winter wildlife food.

Trees for tomorrow

Even a single tree in a garden is enormously helpful to wildlife. It takes many years for a young tree to grow, but if you have the chance to plant one today you'll be helping the wildlife of the future.

A single tree, such as this beech, can be home to furry animals, birds and hundreds of bugs.

Gardening for wildlife

Almost every flower or bush is useful to wildlife, although some types are better than others. The best kind of wildlife garden has plants of many sizes, shapes and species.

Local plants

Wildlife tends to be most attracted to native plants, which come from the country where you live. These grow more easily than non-natives, because the local soil and climate suit them better.

All of these flowers are native to Britain.

The wild side

Most native flowers are what people call wild flowers – types that spread naturally without being planted. You can buy seeds if you want to grow particular kinds, though.

Field poppy

Teasel

St John's wort

*

*

*

Ox-eye daisy

Just for show

Many kinds of flowers on sale in garden centres and shops are ornamental varieties. These have been specially bred to look good, but over time, they have lost many of their natural features. Most have no nectar or scent, and some don't even make pollen, so they're not very useful to wildlife.

Mix it up

Don't worry if you have a lot of non-native flowers in your garden. It's fine to have them too, as some kinds are useful to wildlife. The most important thing is variety.

Insects visit sunflowers for their nectar. *

Forget-me-not

These non-natives are good for a wildlife garden.

A foxglove's pattern of spots guides bees to the nectar inside.

Cranesbill

Shrubs and bushes

Animals need large plants as well as flowers. If your garden is too small for a native tree, shrubs and bushes provide lots of the same benefits but in a compact form.

The fruits of this guelder rose bush have attracted a hungry mouse.

Many bird species nest in elder bushes or feed on their berries.

Its plump fruits make cotoneaster a great shrub for wildlife.

A butterfly garden

On a summer's day, you're likely to see butterflies flitting around in gardens. You can attract more by growing some of the flowers shown here.

Seasonal selections

Butterflies are out and about from mid March until late September, so a mix of spring, summer and autumn blooming flowers will keep them coming for as long as possible.

Peacock butterflies are active all summer, when these hemp agrimony flowers bloom.

Colour counts

Every type of pollen carrier has favourite flower colours. Butterflies are especially attracted to flowers with purple, pink or white petals.

Brimstone butterfly on aubretia flowers

Buddleias are so popular with butterflies that they're sometimes referred to as butterfly bushes.

What shape?

Generally, butterflies choose small, tube-shaped flowers that they can stand on while they drink nectar. They also visit daisy-like flowers with tiny parts in the middle.

Small copper on Michaelmas daisy

Red admiral on ice plant

Green-veined white on wallflower

The flowers shown below are appealing to butterflies, too.

Phlox

Candytuft

A butterfly puddle

As well as nectar, butterflies need water to stay alive. Some also need chemicals called minerals, which they get from mud puddles. Create a puddle and groups of butterflies might come to rest and drink.

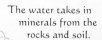

The water takes in minerals from the rocks and soil.

Top up the water from time to time.

1. Bury a large flowerpot all the way up to the rim.

2. Fill it almost to the top with gravel, rocks and a little soil.

3. Add water until a natural puddle forms at the top.

Going wild

Many people work hard to keep their gardens tidy and weed-free, but wildlife thrives in messy areas. If you can, let a corner of your garden grow wild to attract more wildlife.

Rye grass

A mini meadow

Create a mini wildlife meadow by letting a patch of grass grow long, with a few native grasses like the ones shown here. Bugs and small animals live in long grass, and larger animals hunt them.

You might occasionally see a kestrel looking for mice in your meadow.

Annual meadow grass

What is a weed?

Some people say weeds are bad, but others say they're good plants that are growing in the wrong place. It's certainly true that many plants that are described as weeds are helpful to wildlife.

A patch of nettles in the corner of a garden offers butterflies a place to lay eggs.

Brambles provide animals with shelter and tasty berries.

Peacock butterfly

Dandelions attract bees, and some types of birds too.

Weed control

You need to be careful when growing weeds, as they can spread quickly and even harm other plants. Try not to let any grow outside your wild area.

Goose grass is sticky, smelly and not much use to wildlife, so keep it out of the garden.

Wood piles

Old tree branches, logs and dead leaves needn't be burned or thrown away. Put them in a pile where they won't be disturbed, and they might become home to bugs, slimy creatures, or even a hibernating hedgehog.

Stag beetles lay eggs in rotten wood piles. The larvae live there for many years.

A fruity feast

If you have a fruit tree, don't clear away the ripe fruits that fall from it in autumn. A few left on the lawn will soon be eaten by bugs, birds or mammals such as foxes.

This wasp is sucking the sweet juices from a fallen plum.

Harmony with nature

"Organic" is a word which describes living things. Organic gardens rely on nature rather than man-made chemicals to grow well, so they're good for wildlife.

Healthy soil

Certain plants, such as beans, sweet peas and lupins, turn nitrogen from the air into food for soil. Growing them helps to keep soil and other plants healthy. You can also feed garden soil with compost, a rich mixture of rotting waste, instead of man-made chemical plant foods. (There's more about compost on pages 310-311.)

Plants like this sweet pea are both pretty and good for gardens.

Natural pest control

All gardeners want to protect their plants from pests and disease, and many use pesticides to do this. Nature has its own solution, though, in the shape of other garden animals that will eat pests. Encourage them to live in your garden, if you can.

Greenfly are notorious garden pests, but they're no match for this hungry ladybird.

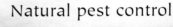

Helper plants

You can keep plants healthy with the help of another plant. The helper will either repel pests or attract the animals that eat them. Blackfly, for instance, eat tomato plants. But planting French marigolds between the tomato plants gets rid of the blackfly, which don't like the marigolds' scent.

Marigolds repel many types of garden pests.

These strong-smelling herbs are helper plants.

Rosemary

Garlic

A hands-on approach

A good wildlife garden needs a certain number of weeds, but they can take over if you let them. Digging them up by hand is safer for animals and the soil than using weedkiller.

Bindweed is a harmful weed, because it spreads far and fast. Pull it out whenever you see it.

Not all bad

Before you declare war on all the unwanted plants and animals in the garden, remember that everything has some role to play in nature. Although they're a nuisance to you, they could be a vital meal to a starving animal.

Today's plant-chewing caterpillar is tomorrow's pollen-carrying butterfly.

Slugs destroy garden plants, but they're also dinner for hungry hedgehogs.

Soil food

Compost is a mixture of natural things, such as dead plants, which are slowly rotting. A compost heap may not be pretty, but it has many benefits for your garden.

Natural recycling

Plants and animals are still full of useful chemicals after they die. The natural process of decay, helped by living things such as worms, allows these chemicals to be set free. This is what happens in a compost heap.

* Fungi are plant-like growths that break down rotting matter.

* Earthworms help to turn rotted matter into a useful mixture.

Why make compost?

Mixing compost with your soil makes it richer, helping plants to grow well without needing artificial plant food. Keeping a compost heap is also a good way to use things which would normally be thrown away, such as kitchen waste. There are lots of things you can add to a heap.

Plant matter such as vegetables and leaves is good for compost. You can also use grass clippings or old teabags.

Don't add meat scraps – they encourage rats.

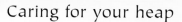

Caring for your heap

You can keep compost in a pile, but it's better to use a container such as a dustbin, with holes in the bottom for drainage. This helps it to stay warm and rot more quickly. To keep the compost healthy and stop it from smelling, you need to water it and turn it over with a garden fork from time to time.

Compost community

Compost is not only excellent soil food, it's also a magnet for wildlife. Shortly after you start a compost heap, you'll see lots of living things start to move in.

The simplest compost heap is a pile of rotting things in a corner of the garden.

House crickets lay their eggs on compost and rubbish heaps.

The Devil's coach-horse is one of many types of beetles that live in compost.

Amphibians such as this toad are drawn to the warmth and damp of compost, as well as its tasty worms.

Wildlife in danger

Many wild animals are struggling to survive. People harm their food supplies and destroy the safe places where they breed, but there are things you can do to protect them.

Alien invaders

Some native animals are threatened by non-native (alien) species, which are fiercer, or better able to survive. Grey squirrels, for instance, compete with their red relatives for food and breeding places. If red squirrels live in your area, you could help them by buying a squirrel feeder which greys are too heavy to use.

American grey squirrels carry a disease which is lethal to the UK's native reds.

Because of grey squirrels, red squirrels like this might one day die out in Britain.

Problem plants

Although some non-native plants are good for wildlife, a few types can damage the natural balance. They take water and space from native plants and may even breed with them, creating a hybrid – a new plant that's a mix of the two. Sometimes, the hybrids replace the natives.

Wild bluebells like these are under threat from Spanish varieties.

No place to go

Huge numbers of natural habitats, such as moors, are being replaced by farmland and houses. As a result, frogs, hedgehogs and many insects are being squeezed out of the wild. In some cases, gardens are their only hope.

Over half of the UK's 60 native butterfly species are threatened by a lack of overgrown land.

Comma butterfly *

High brown fritillary *

Poison peril

Poison is a serious problem for many animals. Farmers often spray crops with chemicals to destroy pests, but this affects the animals that feed on them too. They are left with nothing to eat, or even killed by eating the poisoned bugs.

The more insects are poisoned, the fewer will be left for insect-eating birds such as swallows.

Hazards at home

Even in a garden, animals can find themselves in danger. Prowling pets, weedkiller, slug pellets and garden bonfires are all potential hazards for local wildlife.

Cats kill garden birds. A pet cat should be fitted with a collar and bell, so birds can hear it coming.

Always check wood and leaf piles for sleeping hedgehogs before lighting a bonfire.

Making space

If you have very little space in your garden, or no garden at all, there are still quick and easy things you can do for wildlife.

Sink and swim

An old enamel sink, cat litter tray or similar container can easily become a mini wildlife pond. Just place it in a sunny spot and fill it with water. Add a few stones, so animals can climb in and out easily.

If you have room, add a small water plant or two, such as this starwort.

Stones

Butterflies might come to rest on an ivy-covered wall in the sun.

Climbing plants

You can use house or garden walls to grow climbing plants such as ivy. These provide wildlife with berries in winter and shelter all year round.

A hidey-hole

A piece of wood or corrugated iron propped up against the side of a shed or wall might be all you need to make a welcome hidey-hole for small animals. Make sure the iron has no sharp corners or edges.

Small animals, such as toads, tend to shelter in the shadows beneath things.

Plants in pots

If you haven't much ground for planting, you could grow things in pots instead. A small shrub or a few flowers and herbs will attract more visitors than you might think.

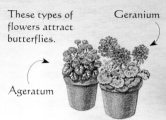

These types of flowers attract butterflies.

Ageratum

Geranium

Bees are attracted by the smell of catmint.

A window box

Even without a garden, it's still possible to help garden wildlife. Window boxes or glass-mounted bird feeders don't need any ground at all.

Plants like these in a window box will attract pollen carriers.

Snowdrop

Crocus

Grape hyacinth

Get involved

Another way to help wildlife is to join a local conservation group. You can find contact details for some groups on the Usborne Quicklinks Website at www.usborne-quicklinks.com.

This feeder has suction cups so you can stick it to a window. It's an ideal way to see birds close up.

INDEX

PHOTO CREDITS (t = top, m = middle, b = bottom, l = left, r = right)

ACKNOWLEDGEMENTS

ILLUSTRATORS Dave Ashby, Mike Atkinson, Graham Austin, Bob Bampton, John Barber, David Baxter, Andrew Becket, Joyce Bee, Isabel Bowring, Trevor Boyer, Wendy Bramall, Paul Brooks, Mark Burgess, Hilary Burn, Liz Butler, Kuo Kang Chen, Frankie Coventry, Patrick Cox, Christina Darter, Kevin Dean, Sarah De Ath, Peter Dennis, Brin Edwards, Michelle Emblem, Sandra Fernandez, Denise Finney, Wayne Forde, Don Forrest, Sarah Fox-Davies, John Francis, Nigel Frey, Sheila Galbraith, Toby Gibson, Will Giles, Victoria Goaman, Victoria Gordon, Alan Harris, Nick Harris, Tim Hayward, Christine Howes, Roy Hutchinson, David Hurrell, Ian Jackson, Elaine Keenan, Roger Kent, Aziz Khan, Colin King, Deborah King, Steven Kirk, Jonathan Langley, Ken Lilly, Stephen Lings, Mick Loates, Rachel Lockwood, Kevin Lyles, Alan Marks, Andy Martin, Rodney Matthews, Uwe Mayer, Rob McCraig, Joseph McEwan, Malcom McGregor, Dee McLean, Ian McNee, David Mead, Richard Millington, Annabel Milne, David More, Dee Morgan, Robert Morton, David Nash, Tricia Newell, Barbara Nicholson, Richard Orr, David Palmer, Charles Pearson, Julie Piper, Gillian Platt, Maurice Pledger, Cynthia Pow, David Quinn, Charles Raymond, Barry Raynor, Michelle Ross, Chris Shields, John Sibbick, Maggie Silver, Gwen Simpson, Peter Stebbing, Ralph Stobart, Petula Stone, Elena Temporin, George Thompson, Joan Thompson, John Thompson-Steinkrauss, Ron Tiner, Joyce Tuhill, Sally Volke, Ian Wallace, Phil Weare, Gerald Wood, John Woodcock, James Woods, David Wright and John Yates

Managing designer: Karen Tomlins
Cover design: Joanne Kirkby
Additional designs: Reuben Barrance
Artwork co-ordinator: Louise Breen
Website advisor: Lisa Watts
Additional thanks to Mike Olley, and Steve Wills
of the Royal National Lifeboat Association